ECONOMIC AND SOCIAL JUSTICE

A Human Rights Perspective

HUMAN RIGHTS EDUCATION SERIES

Topic Book 1

By

DAVID A. SHIMAN

The Human Rights Education Series is published by the Human Rights Resource Center at
the University of Minnesota and the Stanley Foundation. The series provides resources for the
ever-growing body of educators and activists working to build a culture of human rights in the
United States and throughout the world.

The Human Rights Education Series is edited by Nancy Flowers.
Book design by Terri Kinne.
Illustrations for this book were taken from *The Art of Rini Templeton*
(The Real Comet Press, Seattle, Washington, 1987).

ISBN 0-9675334-0-6

To order further copies of *Economic and Social Justice: A Human Rights Perspective*, contact:

Human Rights Resource Center
University of Minnesota
229 - 19th Avenue South, Room 439
Minneapolis, MN 55455
Tel: 1-888-HREDUC8   Fax: 612-625-2011
email: humanrts@tc.umn.edu
http://www.hrusa.org *and* http://www.umn.edu/humanrts

A contribution to the United Nations Decade for Human Rights Education, 1995-2004

TABLE OF CONTENTS

In a real sense, all life is interrelated. The agony of the poor impoverishes the rich; the betterment of the poor enriches the rich. We are inevitably our brother's keepers because we are our brother's brother. Whatever affects one directly affects all indirectly.

Martin Luther King

ACKNOWLEDGMENTS

When most people in the United States are asked about human rights, they talk of the right to vote and the Bill of Rights, particularly the freedoms of speech, press, religion, and assembly. Many have defended these powerful freedoms on behalf of their country, their neighbors, and themselves.

There are other rights declared in the United Nations' Universal Declaration of Human Rights (UDHR) that are not part of the human rights consciousness of most Americans. These include rights to adequate food, clothing, housing, medical care, and even education. They also include rights related to social security, marriage and family, and labor union participation and working conditions. These are among the social, economic, and cultural rights identified in Articles 16 and 22-29 of the UDHR to which everyone is entitled, regardless of who you are or where you live.

Social and Economic Justice: A Human Rights Perspective is intended to expand the conversation about human rights. It provides background information, ideas for taking action, and interactive activities to help people think about human rights in a broader, more inclusive manner. It strives to help us define issues like homelessness, poverty, hunger, and inadequate health care, not only as "social or economic problems," but also as human rights challenges.

Placing problems such as these within the human rights framework provided by the UDHR incorporates a moral vision into public policy and personal decision making. It provides a rationale for action in the name of human dignity, peace, and justice. This publication is the *Human Rights Education Series – Topic Book 1,* a companion to *Human Rights Here and Now: Celebrating the Universal Declaration of Human Rights.* That book is broader in scope, while *Social and Economic Justice: A Human Rights Perspective* focuses on those rights found principally in the last third of the UDHR. Both books are tools for bringing the UDHR into the lives of people in the United States.

Both books are also contributions to the United Nations Decade for Human Rights Education, 1995-2004. They imagine a world in which everyone learns about these human rights and accepts as a personal responsibility to advocate for and defend them on behalf of oneself and one's community: local, national, and global. It is a powerful vision.

◆ ◆ ◆

This book is the outcome of contributions from many educators and institutions committed to human rights goals. There are some who deserve special mention.

Those who contributed activities or essays:

- Alameda County Community Food Bank (sections of *Hunger USA*), Nancy Flowers *(Martin Luther King – From Civil Rights to Human Rights)*, Shulamith Koenig *(Economic, Social and Cultural Rights: Questions and Answers)*, and the Resource Center of the Americas (sections of *Wages, Earning Power, Profit, and Responsibility)*.

Those who served as principal authors of activities or essays:

- Sushanna Ellington *(The Elderly Poor)* and Gwen Willems *(Economic, Social, and Cultural Rights as Human Rights: Historical Background)*.

Those who were co-authors:

- Kristi Rudelius-Palmer *(Taking the Human Rights Temperature of Your School)*, Sherry Kempf *(Economic Justice: The Scramble for Wealth and Power)*, and Karen Kraco *(Community Research and Action Plan: Social and Economic Rights)*.

Those who offered editorial suggestions:

- Elise Guyette, Janet Schmidt, Patrick Manson, and the more than forty educators participating in human rights workshops organized by Amnesty International USA and the Vermont Alliance for the Social Studies.

Nancy Flowers for the keen editorial eye and hand that touched every page of this book and for her tireless encouragement and assistance.

Amnesty International USA for fostering human rights education and supporting the Human Rights Educators' Network of dedicated volunteers.

The Stanley Foundation, Joan Winship and Jill Goldesberry, for their support in the creation and publication of this book.

The Human Rights Resource Center at the University of Minnesota, Terri Kinne, Betsy Clink, Jennifer Saari, and Kristi Rudelius-Palmer for their coordination, editing, and design expertise in the final production stage.

Center for World Education, College of Education and Social Services, University of Vermont for hosting the initial writing and research institute in July 1977.

Shulamith Koenig for her vision of the UN Decade for Human Rights Education, 1995-2004.

◆ ◆ ◆

Five publications in particular made substantial contributions to this book.

- David Shiman, *Teaching Human Rights* (Center for Teaching International Relations, University of Denver, 1998).

- *Educating for Economic Justice. Human Rights Education: The Fourth R* (Human Rights Educators' Network, Amnesty International USA) Vol. 9:1 (Spring, 1998).

- Alicia Dorosin, Courtney Geelan, Eve Gordon, and Rachel Moore, *Why Is There Hunger in Our Community?* (Alameda County Community Food Bank, Oakland, CA, 1997).

- Amy Sanders and Meredith Sommers, *Child Labor Is Not Cheap* (Resource Center of the Americas, Minneapolis, MN, 1997).

- Nancy Flowers (ed.) *Human Rights Here and Now: Celebrating the Universal Declaration of Human Rights* (Human Rights Educators' Network, Amnesty International USA, Minneapolis, MN, 1998).

USING *ECONOMIC AND SOCIAL JUSTICE*

On December 10, 1998 the world celebrated the 50th anniversary of the United Nations' Universal Declaration of Human Rights (UDHR).

The United States was instrumental in creating the UDHR, with Eleanor Roosevelt as head of the drafting committee and the US Constitution as a principal model. The USA joined the UN General Assembly in unanimously adopting the UDHR, accepting its exhortation that "every individual and every organ of society" should "strive by teaching and education to promote respect for these rights and freedoms."

Americans, through our Constitution with its Amendments, already possess many of the political and civil rights articulated in the UDHR. However, the UDHR goes further than the US Constitution, including many social and economic rights as well. The UDHR's Article 25, in particular, guarantees everyone has a human right to "a standard of living adequate for the health and well-being of himself and of his family, including food, clothing, housing and medical care and necessary social services." However, when most people debate issues of hunger, housing, and health care, for example, they rarely frame these as human rights questions. Americans tend to equate civil/political rights with human rights.

Economic and Social Justice: A Human Rights Perspective addresses the social and economic rights found in Articles 16 and 22 through 27 of the UDHR, which are generally not recognized as human rights in the United States. These rights were further articulated in the 1966 International Covenant on Economic, Social and Cultural Rights (ICESCR). Although in 1948 the United States was a signatory to the non-binding Universal Declaration, it remains among the few nations that have not ratified the ICESCR.

In keeping with the UDHR and ICESCR, *Economic and Social Justice: A Human Rights Perspective* treats social and economic rights as inalienable human rights, putting them in both local and global perspective and illustrating the interdependence between social/economic and civil/political rights.

Economic and Social Justice: A Human Rights Perspective is also built on the premise that the study of human rights is also a call to action. Therefore, the activities briefly described below suggest ways in which participants can act to make this a better world.

Economic and Social Justice: A Human Rights Perspective begins with a brief history of economic, social, and cultural rights and an essay, in question and answer format, that introduces these rights. Although cultural rights are interrelated and of equal importance as economic and social rights, this book primarily addresses justice regarding economic and social components.

Part II provides nine activities to further explore and learn about social and economic rights:

- **Activity 1**, *Imagine a Country*, introduces social and economic rights in an engaging and provocative manner;

- **Activity 2**, *Economic Justice: The Scramble for Wealth and Power*, provides a lively exploration of fair distribution of wealth;

- **Activity 3**, *Wages, Earning Power, Profit, and Responsibility: International Lessons*, makes a powerful connection between wages and working conditions abroad and responsible consumerism at home;

- **Activity 4**, *Community Research and Action Plan: Economic and Social Rights*, targets human rights challenges in the community;

- **Activity 5**, *Hunger USA* is a multi-part lesson that explores links between hunger and poverty;

- **Activity 6**, *The Elderly Poor* uses case studies to highlight human rights concerns;

- **Activity 7**, *Taking the Human Rights Temperature of Your School* employs a questionnaire;

- **Activity 8**, *Martin Luther King Jr. – From Civil Rights to Human Rights*, introduces King's broader global human rights vision;

- **Activity 9**, *Activists for Human Rights* identifies historical figures in US history who have championed human rights and have a particular focus on social and economic rights.

The Appendix contains documents, a glossary of terms, a directory of resource organizations, and a bibliography to assist those eager to increase their understanding and/or move into action to address social and economic rights.

In the future days which we seek to make secure, we look forward to a world founded upon four essential freedoms.

The first is freedom of speech and expression – everywhere in the world.

The second is the freedom of every person to worship God in his own way – everywhere in the world.

The third is the freedom from want, which, translated into world terms, means economic understanding which will secure to every nation a healthy peacetime life for its inhabitants – everywhere in the world.

The fourth is freedom from fear, which, translated into world terms, means a world-wide reduction of armaments to such a point and in such a thorough fashion that no nation will be in a position to commit an act of physical aggression against any neighbor – anywhere in the world. It is a definite bias for a kind of world attainable in our own time and generation.

Franklin D. Roosevelt
State of the Union Address
January 6, 1941

PART I:

Economic, Social, and Cultural Rights Fundamentals

> *[R]ecognition of the inherent dignity and of the equal and inalienable rights of all members of the human family is the foundation of freedom, justice, and peace in the world.*
>
> Preamble, Universal Declaration of Human Rights

PART I CONTENTS:

> *Widespread poverty and concentrated wealth cannot long endure side by side with democracy.*
>
> Thomas Jefferson

ECONOMIC, SOCIAL, AND CULTURAL RIGHTS AS HUMAN RIGHTS: HISTORICAL BACKGROUND

Long before human rights were written down in international documents and national constitutions, people revealed their commitment to principles of propriety, justice, and caring through cultural practices and oral traditions. Basic rights and responsibilities, such as the right to food and the golden rule of "Do unto others as you would have them do unto you," revolved around family, tribe, religion, class, community, or state.

The Foundation of Economic, Social, and Cultural Rights

The earliest attempts of literate societies to write about rights and responsibilities date back more than 4,000 years to the Babylonian Code of Hammurabi. This Code, the Old and New Testaments of the Bible, the Analects of Confucius, the Koran, and the Hindu Vedas are five of the oldest written sources which address questions of people's duties, rights, and responsibilities. In addition, the Inca and Aztec codes of conduct and justice and the Iroquois Constitution are Native American sources dating back well before the eighteenth century. Other pre-World War II documents, such as the English Bill of Rights, the US Constitution and Bill of Rights, and the French Declaration of the Rights of Man and the Citizen, focused on civil and political rights. They concentrated on the rights of citizens to equality, liberty, and due process and of participation in the political life of their community and society through activities such as voting.

At the end of World War II, citizens working through *nongovernmental organizations* urged the creators of the United Nations system to include the promotion of a spectrum of human rights in the *UN Charter*. These are rights to which all people are entitled, regardless of who they are or where they live. The United Nations created a *Commission on Human Rights* in 1946. Forcefully led by Eleanor Roosevelt, the Commission drafted the *Universal Declaration of Human Rights (UDHR)*. It includes fundamental rights to life, liberty, and security as well as a broad range of civil, political, economic, social, and cultural rights.

On December 10, 1948, the Universal Declaration of Human Rights was adopted unanimously by 48 members of the United Nations, with eight countries abstaining.

Today, the promotion of human rights is guided by what is referred to as the *International Bill of Rights*. It includes the UDHR and two *treaties*—the *International*

---

* This and other terms indicated in bold italic type are defined in *A Human Rights Glossary*, p. 99.

Covenant on Civil and Political Rights and the *International Covenant on Economic, Social, and Cultural Rights*. These treaties elaborate on rights identified in the UDHR and, when adopted by individual states, have the force of law. Each treaty provides for independent experts who monitor governments and requires periodic reporting by governments to ensure that they are following treaty provisions.

Economic, social, and cultural rights, are specified in Articles 16 and 22-29 of the UDHR. They identify an impressive list of human rights concerns and refer to:

- marriage and family;
- work and leisure (free choice of employment, just conditions of work, equal pay for equal work, just remuneration, freedom to form and join trade unions, and rest);
- a standard of living adequate for food, shelter, clothing, medical care, and social services;
- security in case of unemployment, sickness, disability, widowhood, and old age;
- special care and assistance in motherhood and childhood;
- education (free and compulsory elementary education, equal access based on merit, parental choice, and full development of the human personality);
- participation in the cultural life of one's community;
- protection of one's own literary, scientific, and artistic productions;
- social and international order that enables these human rights to be realized; and
- one's duties to one's community.

Economic, Social, and Cultural Rights in Practice

The United States has long attended to some of these economic, social, and cultural rights. For example, during the Great Depression, President Franklin Delano Roosevelt (FDR) sought to save our struggling economic system and implement his vision of economic and social justice. In a 1937 speech in Chicago, FDR declared, "I see one-third of a nation ill-housed, ill-clad, and ill-nourished... The test of our progress is not whether we add more to the abundance of those who have much; it is whether we provide enough for those who have too little." Four years later, in his State of the Union Address, FDR spoke inspiringly of a world with four major freedoms—freedom of speech and religion and freedom from want and fear (See p. vi).

During Roosevelt's presidency and in the years since, the United States has sought to respond to these economic and social needs with new policies. These have included health insurance programs, social security insurance, unemployment insurance, public works projects, farm supports, expanded educational opportunities, and laws supporting worker rights to organize and strike. However, US government leaders have never presented these to the American people as human rights to which everyone is entitled.

During the years after World War II, the Cold War polarized capitalist and communist countries into East and West, with each emphasizing different types of rights. The United States, proud of its achievements in the areas of civil and political rights, criticized its communist rivals, particularly the Soviet Union, for denying these to their citizens. On its part, the USSR asserted the importance of government in ensuring that all citizens have adequate food, health care, employment, social insurance, and education. Members of the Soviet Union accused the USA of refusing to guarantee these economic and social rights to its citizens. These political stances, however, did not adequately capture the reality that both sides of the East-West conflict were struggling with issues related to the full range of rights.

Other nations, such as Sweden and Denmark, sought to promote both clusters of rights through the establishment of social welfare states. And many of the new nations in Africa and Asia, created since the end of World War II, such as Egypt, the Philippines, South Africa, and Tanzania, wrote constitutions embodying the wide range of principles found in the UDHR. They have sought to establish development strategies reflecting a commitment to these rights.

However, as we look across the globe, it is evident that we are far from achieving the goals of justice and human dignity for all. Yes, there have been popular movements towards democratization in many parts of the world, with elected leaders replacing dictators. Yes, there have been advances in education, health care, and sanitation. Nevertheless, among the 4.4 billion people who live in developing countries, three-fifths still have no access to basic sanitation, almost one-third are without safe drinking water, one-quarter lack adequate housing, one-fifth live beyond reach of modern health services, one-fifth of the children do not reach grade five in school, and one-fifth are undernourished.

Almost all of the world's nations have indicated a commitment to achieving full economic, social, and cultural rights by agreeing to the United Nations' international covenant on these rights. The United States has not; it appears unwilling to conduct the self-scrutiny that would be required.

The results of this lack of commitment leave the United States with much to do. One US child in five lives in official poverty, between 1.2 and 2 million people are homeless during any year, 40 million are without health insurance, and the number of people turning to emergency food shelves and soup kitchens for their meals is rapidly growing.

Human rights are **universal**, **indivisible**, **interdependent**, and **inalienable**. Therefore, the enhancement of all rights—civil, political, economic, social, and cultural—must be our goal.

SOURCE: Written by Gwen Willems, College of Education and Human Development, University of Minnesota, and David Shiman, Center for World Education, University of Vermont.

ECONOMIC, SOCIAL, AND CULTURAL RIGHTS: QUESTIONS AND ANSWERS

? **What, in general, do we mean by "economic, social, and cultural rights"?**

"Human rights" is an expression that covers a wide range of aspects of human existence considered essential for life in dignity and security. Some of these relate to the freedom of the individual to act as she or he pleases as long as that action does not infringe on the rights and freedoms of others. These liberty-oriented rights are usually called *civil and political rights* and include freedom of speech and religion, the right to fair trial, and the right to be free from torture and arbitrary arrest. Other rights relate to conditions necessary to meet basic human needs, such as food, shelter, education, health care, and gainful employment. These are called *economic, social and cultural rights*.

? **Which are more important: economic, social, and cultural rights or civil and political rights?**

All rights—civil, cultural, economic, political, and social—are considered *"universal, indivisible, interdependent* and *interrelated"* (1993 Vienna Declaration and Program of Action, Part I, paragraph 5). When considered together, these rights basically address the human being, whoever he or she is, as a whole person free from fear and free from want. In the USA, when people speak of rights, they often stress the civil and political rights guaranteed citizens by the US Constitution and its Amendments. In countries where the basic needs of individuals are not fulfilled and for groups of people discriminated against in certain countries, social and economic rights are often of primary concern.

In all societies, both types of rights are integrally related. People who are denied civil and political rights have no means of protecting the economic, social, and cultural rights that guarantee them their basic needs. Similarly, in a society where basic survival needs are not met, civil and political rights are meaningless if an individual must first be concerned with obtaining adequate food, shelter, and health care.

The interdependence and importance of rights extend to the global level. Violations of social, economic, and cultural rights are responsible for patterns of increased income disparity and economic exploitation.

? Which economic, social, and cultural rights are guaranteed in international human rights documents?

In the *Universal Declaration of Human Rights* (UDHR), Article 16 and Articles 22 through 27 encompass economic, social, and cultural rights.

> **Article 16** of the UDHR sets forth the right to marry, to have free choice in marriage, and to found a family.

> **Article 22** states "Everyone is entitled to the realization of the economic, social and cultural rights indispensable for his dignity." Article 23 articulates the right to work, to choose employment, and to form labor unions.

> **Article 24** sets forth the right to rest and leisure and of reasonable limitation of working hours.

> **Article 25** includes a person's right to a "standard of living adequate for the health and well-being of himself and of his family, including food, clothing, housing and medical care and necessary social services."

> **Article 26** states that individuals have the right to education, free and compulsory at the elementary level, with technical and professional education generally available, and higher education equally accessible on the basis of merit.

> **Article 27** describes the right to freely participate in the cultural life of the community, to enjoy the arts, and to share in scientific advancement.

> **Article 28 and 29** include the right to a social and international order that enables these rights to be realized and refers to one's duties to one's community.

These rights are further elaborated in the *International Covenant on Economic, Social and Cultural Rights*. They are also articulated in specialized human rights treaties such as the *Convention on the Rights of the Child* (CRC) and the *Convention on the Elimination of All Forms of Discrimination Against Women* (CEDAW), *treaties* that focus on the needs of particularly disadvantaged, marginalized, and vulnerable groups of people all over the world.

? Do any of these human rights documents have the force of law?

The Universal Declaration is a resolution of the General Assembly of the United Nations, which creates a high expectation that it will be taken seriously. However, a *declaration* does not create obligations that are technically binding in law. Nevertheless, since the Universal Declaration is so widely used as the primary statement of what are considered human rights today, it is often regarded as having legal significance and considered *"customary" international law* and as the authentic interpretation of the references in the *UN Charter*.

The specific rights in the UDHR have been *codified* into the International Covenant on Economic, Social, and Cultural Rights (ICESCR) and the *International Covenant on Civil and Political Rights* (ICCPR). A *covenant* is a *treaty* which, under the rules of international law, creates legal obligations on all states that *ratify* it. Similarly, the Convention on the Rights of the Child (CRC) and Convention on the Elimination of all forms of Discrimination Against Women (CEDAW) also are treaties that are binding on the *states* that ratify them.

Therefore, citizens worldwide should put pressure on their governments to ratify these treaties and to abide by the obligations they set forth. For example, a right to health care is mandated by the ICESCR, meaning that a basic and adequate health care entitlement should be guaranteed to all citizens and residents of countries ratifying the treaty.

? **Not all countries are in equal positions to provide for their citizens. How is this dealt with in the International Covenant on Economic, Social, and Cultural Rights (ICESCR)?**

The ICESCR states that each *state party* to the covenant should "undertake steps, individually and through international assistance and cooperation, especially economic and technical, to the maximum of its available resources, with a view to achieving progressively the full realization of the rights recognized in the Covenant, by all appropriate means, including particularly the adoption of legislative measures."

It also states that state parties must guarantee these rights without discrimination with respect to race, color, sex, language, religion, political or other opinion, and social status.

? **Is the United States a party to the International Covenant on Economic, Social and Cultural Rights?**

No. The United States *signed* the Covenant in 1979 under the Carter administration but is not fully bound by it until it is ratified. For political reasons, the Carter administration did not push for the necessary review of the Covenant by the Senate, which must give its "advice and consent" before the US can ratify a treaty. The Reagan and Bush administrations took the view that economic, social, and cultural rights were not really rights but merely desirable social goals and therefore should not be the object of binding treaties. The Clinton Administration has not denied the nature of these rights but has not found it politically expedient to engage in a battle with Congress over the Covenant. If the Covenant were to be considered at this point in time, it would likely result either in the defeat of ratification or in accompanying the ratification with reservations that would empty it of any meaningful obligations. Several organizations in the USA mobilized community groups to put pressure on the Congress to ratify the ICESCR in connection with the 50th anniversary of the UDHR in 1998.

? Although the US has not ratified the ICESCR, does it have any obligations as a signatory of this Covenant?

Yes. According to the law of treaties, a government that has signed but not ratified a treaty (like the Covenant) must "refrain from acts which would defeat the object and purpose of [the] treaty...until it shall have made its intention clear not be become a party ...." Unfortunately, courts in the USA are not likely to attach much importance to this rule if an action were brought before that claims the USA is defeating the object and purpose of the Covenant.

? What would it mean to ordinary people if the US Senate gave its advice and consent and the USA ratified the Covenant?

It would mean four things:

1. The USA would be required to "take steps...to the maximum of its available resources, with a view to achieving progressively the full realization of the rights recognized" in the Covenant.

2. The USA must ensure that the rights in the Covenant are enjoyed without discrimination based on race, color, sex, religion, political or other opinion, national or social origin, property, birth or other status. (In most countries, "other status" includes disability and in some countries also refers to sexual orientation.)

3. The USA would be required to report to the UN Committee on Economic, Social and Cultural Rights on measures adopted and progress made in achieving the observance of the Covenant rights. The 18-member Committee, on which a US expert could have a seat if elected, would examine this report and pose questions. The Committee would then formulate its general observations on how the USA might do better, if it concludes that the USA is not doing enough to realize the rights in the Covenant.

4. Finally, the rights in the Covenant would become part of the "Supreme Law of the Land; and the Judges in every State shall be bound thereby," according to Article VI, Clause 2 of the US Constitution. Thus, in theory, anyone whose rights under the Covenant were violated would be able to bring a case before the courts.

In practice, however, the courts could decide that the treaty is not the kind it can apply without implementing legislation from Congress ("non-self-executing treaty") or, and this is more likely, the Senate would add a reservation to the US ratification excluding the possibility for citizens to invoke the Covenant before the courts of the United States.

? In addition to the legal ramifications of the Covenant, in what other ways can its provisions effectively be used to address social and economic concerns?

Whether or not persons whose economic, social and cultural rights were not ensured could go to court, the Covenant still would articulate a legitimate standard to which social justice movements could refer to in holding the federal government accountable. The Covenant also can serve as a tool for planning insofar as it sets out the basic rights that cannot be denied in the process of seeking other social goals. It is widely acknowledged that integrating the human rights framework in the struggles to alleviate poverty, hunger, homelessness, and unequal educational opportunities empowers individuals and communities to assert and claim social and economic justice.

Source: Adapted from *Human Rights Education: The Fourth R*, 9:1 (Spring 1998), a publication of Amnesty International USA's Huma Rights Educators' Network. Original work was written by Shulamith Koenig and the staff of The People's Decade for Human Rights Education (1998), 526 West 111th Street, Suite 4E, New York, NY USA 10025. Web site: http://www.pdhre.org.

PART II:

Activities

> *Necessitous men are not free men.*
>
> Franklin Delano Roosevelt

PART II CONTENTS:

ACTIVITY 1

IMAGINE A COUNTRY

This activity introduces social and economic rights found in the Universal Declaration of Human Rights. It employs rights-related statistics to promote critical reflection on strengths, weaknesses, and contradictions in US society. This multidisciplinary approach encourages participants to draw on the arts, social studies, math, and language arts to express their understanding of and feelings about what they encounter.

Time:	30-60 minutes
Materials:	• Copies of Universal Declaration of Human Rights (UDHR)
	• Copies of summary version of the International Covenant on Economic, Social, and Cultural Rights (ICESCR)
	• Handout 1, *Imagine a Country*
Setting:	Middle school – Adult groups

PROCEDURE

The activity might move in many different directions, depending on participant interest and strengths. It is essential, however, that participants develop a basic understanding of social and economic rights and the international documents in which these rights are articulated.

1. Distribute Handout 1, *Imagine a Country* to participants and ask different participants to read each of the discrete statements. **Note:** Do not indicate that each statement is about the United States.

2. After the reading, allow a brief time for free flowing participant reactions prior to focusing their attention on some of the tasks and questions below.

Questions to consider:

• Are you surprised, disturbed, proud, pleased, or _____ (select your adjective) by any of these statistics in particular?

• Do you have questions about any of the data presented in the essay?

- Do you think this statistical evidence is biased and misrepresents your country? Which statistics in particular are you concerned about?

- How do you explain the apparent contradictions, (e.g., richest nation but high percentage of poverty that exist in the United States)?

- For which social and economic rights does the USA appear to be doing well? For which is there need for substantial improvement?

- What is the responsibility of the government to ensure that everyone achieves these human rights as fully as possible? Are there some conditions, such as inadequate nutrition of children, that the government should address and other conditions, such as homelessness of adults, that it shouldn't? What actions might the government take?

- Who besides government should assume responsibilities for addressing human rights problems?

- Are there some conditions for which the statistics suggest that the USA is doing as well as might be expected and others for which we can expect better results? Do you think we can do better? What makes you think the way you do?

Possible Participant Tasks:

1. Match the conditions described in the essay to articles in the UDHR and ICESCR (abbreviated version). Identify social and economic rights found in ICESCR but were not included in the essay.

2. Look for news stories (TV, magazines, and newspapers) that are about these social and economic rights. Create a bulletin board to post these. Keep adding to this bulletin board during the course of your study of social and economic rights.

3. Indicate your understanding of and feelings about one particular statement in *Imagine a Country* in one of the following ways:

   - create a poem, drawing, or song

   - write a letter to a local newspaper

   - educate your community with posters and drawings.

4. Assess the essay as a whole and create one of the following: 1) a "praise poem, drawing, or song" that draws on facts in the essay to paint the United States in the most positive light or 2) a "poem, drawing or song of lament" that focused on those facts that expose the United States in a negative light. Try to explain how both presentations could be true at the same time.

5. Identify "red flag facts." These are data that uncover inequalities in a situation and suggest that there might be unfair treatment involved. However, more information is usually needed before one can conclude that an inequality exists, (e.g., the percentage of males and females pursuing science careers) is the result of unfair treatment. Identify "red flag facts" and discuss what additional information participants would need to gather.

6. Bring these national statistics home by trying to match the statistics provided in Handout 1, *Imagine A Country*, with local statistics for hunger, homelessness, etc.

Source: Written by David Shiman.

> *Each person born into this world has a right to everything he needs. His right, however, is bound up with that of every other creature and gives him no license to grab everything he can without allowing a share for others.*
>
> Dorothy Fuldheim

IMAGINE A COUNTRY

Can You Imagine...

1. A country that is the richest in the world with the highest Gross National Product, but where one out of four children is born into "official poverty," where one out of four of these "officially poor" children lives in a family where one or more parents work full time, year round, and where the "official poverty" line is set well below the actual cost of minimally adequate housing, health care, food, and other necessities.

2. A country that builds schools to educate all its children, but only provides resources for its preschool Head Start Program to enable 40% of the most needy 3-4 year olds to be ready to learn when they enter the school at 6 years, and where its children rank 21st among the 26 industrialized nations in eighth grade math scores.

3. A country that protects over 90% of its children from the diseases of measles, polio, and DPT (diphtheria, pertussis, and tetanus) through immunization, but where almost 70 million people, including 11 million children (through 18 years) have inadequate or no health insurance, and where the infant mortality rate (number of deaths per 1000 prior to 1 year) for black children (15.1) is twice that for whites (7.6).

4. A country that grows enough food to feed all its people and millions more around the world, but where over 30 million (over 10%) are hungry and more than 50% of the food stamp recipients are children and the number of people using food banks and emergency food shelves has increased substantially in recent years.

5. A country that is first in the world in defense spending and in military exports, but last among the 26 industrialized nations in protecting its children against violence and where 1 in 680 is likely to be killed by gunfire before 20 years, a rate twelve times greater than the other industrialized nations, and where over three million children are reported to be abused and neglected yearly.

6. A country that has laws to ensure the right of all workers to organize and join labor unions and strike to achieve their goals, but where workers, such as farm and textile workers, have often been harassed and intimidated when they try to exercise these rights.

7. A country that claims that "justice is blind" and strives to ensure that everyone is fairly treated in its legal system, but where African-Americans, who comprise 14% of the population, make up 52% of those executed and over 40% of those under death sentence.

8. A country that has passed laws protecting its children from unfair, inhumane labor practices, but whose government has done little to block the importation of merchandise produced by exploited child labor and whose citizens purchase billions of dollars of products from elsewhere in the world that are manufactured in factories where children are abused and exploited.

9. A country that strives to provide social security for its senior citizens and has poverty rates for those over 65 years that are lower than for the population as a whole, but where the poverty for females over 65 years is double that for males over 65 years and where the percentage of African- Americans and Latinos over 65 years in poverty is over 2.5 times that for whites over 65 years.

10. A country that thinks of itself as a "land of opportunity" for all, but where 40% of Hispanic and African-American children and only 16% of white children are "officially poor," where full-time work at minimum wage pays below the official poverty line for a family of two and where two out of three workers who earn the minimum wage are women, where living standards are falling for younger generations despite the fact that many young households have two wage earners, fewer children, and better education than their parents.

11. A country that has a government department charged with the task of developing policies and programs to ensure that all are sheltered, but where approximately 3/4 million are homeless on any given day and between 1.2 and 2 million people during any year and where approximately 20% of those seeking emergency shelter fail to secure it due to lack of resources.

CAN YOU IMAGINE THAT THIS COUNTRY IS THE USA?

Inspired by and based on "Imagine a Country" by Holly Sklar, in *Z Magazine* (July/August 1997).

Data Sources: Sklar, H. (1997). "Imagine a Country," *Z Magazine* (July/August); US Department of Commerce, Bureau of the Census, *Statistical Abstract of the United States* (yearly). World Bank, *World Development Report*, NY. Oxford University Press, (yearly). Children's Defense Fund, *State of America's Children* (yearly). UNICEF, *The State of the World's Children* (yearly). Bread for the World, *US Hunger and Poverty Report* (1998)

ECONOMIC JUSTICE: THE SCRAMBLE FOR WEALTH AND POWER

OVERVIEW

The distribution of wealth and power within society usually affects a person's opportunities to achieve full human rights and live a life with dignity. This activity involves the distribution of wealth. It challenges participants to examine the concepts of "fairness" and "responsibility" and reflect on their own actions.

Time:	1 hour
Materials:	100 pennies
	(or 100 peanuts or wrapped candies for younger participants)
Setting:	Elementary school – Adult groups
	(See suggestions for adaptation for young children at end of activity,)

PROCEDURE

Note: Keep in mind the socioeconomic composition of your participant population. Guard against having this activity confirm the existing inequalities in wealth and power.

PART A: The Scramble

1. Explain to participants that in this activity they will distribute the wealth and power of the world among themselves. This wealth is represented by the 100 pennies. There is only one rule: no participant may touch another member of the group at any time.

2. Arrange the room so that participants have a fairly large area to play the game. Have participants stand or sit in a circle and scatter the pennies evenly in the middle of the circle. Withhold three participants from this part of the activity. Distribute mittens for some participants to wear but postpone discussion of reasons for this until debriefing. **Note:** To emphasize that some start off with more than others, consider giving three or four participants five extra pennies to begin with as well as providing them with special scooping shovels.

At the order of GO, have participants (except the three withheld) gather as many pennies as possible without touching one another. **Note:** Penalties for violations of this rule may be needed, such as removal from the game or payment to the person touched.

3. After all the pennies have been collected, have participants report their wealth to the class. Record participants' names and number of pennies on a board or chart paper under three categories:

   1) "GREAT WEALTH AND POWER"
      (those with six or more pennies—the smallest group);

   2) "SOME WEALTH AND POWER"
      (those with three to five pennies—the middle group); and

   3) "LITTLE WEALTH AND POWER"
      (those with two or fewer pennies—the largest group).

4. Remind the group that these pennies represent their wealth and power in the world. The amount they possess will affect their capacity to satisfy their needs (e.g., basic education, adequate food and nutrition, good health care, adequate housing) and wants (e.g. higher education, cars, computers, toys, television and other luxury items). Those participants with six or more pennies will have their basic "needs" and most of their "wants" met; those with three to five pennies will have their basic needs met, and those with two or fewer pennies will have difficulty surviving due to disease, lack of education, malnutrition, and inadequate shelter.

5. Tell participants that they may, if they wish, give pennies to others; however, they are not required to do so. Tell them that those who do share will be honored as "DONORS," with their names placed on the board. Allow a few minutes for participants to redistribute the pennies if they wish. Then ask for the names of those who gave away pennies and the amount each gave. List them on the board or chart entitled "DONORS." Ask if anyone changed category as a result of giving or receiving pennies and record these shifts on the chart.

6. Explain that some people in their country (and perhaps in their community) and in every country around the globe lack adequate necessities, such as food, education, health care, and shelter. Point out that others, often in the same community or country, are able to acquire almost everything they need and want.

PART B: Creating Economic "Fairness"

1. Divide participants into groups according to the number of pennies they have. Distribute those three participants withheld from the original "scramble" randomly among the different groups. Make note of their reactions to being placed in one group rather than another but save discussion of their placement until the debriefing session.

2. Give each group the task of creating a plan for the fair distribution of the pennies (the world's wealth). Each group should prepare to: a) show why their plan is fair, b) explain what needs to be done (if anything), and c) describe what the group plans to do and why. Give the groups ten minutes to devise their plans.

3. Ask each group to appoint a spokesperson to explain their plan to the others and answer questions. After the plans have been presented and discussed, announce that a vote will now be held on which plan to adopt.

4. When participants are ready to vote, announce the following: Participants with six or more pennies have five votes, those with three to five pennies have two votes, and those with two or fewer pennies have one-half vote. This strategy reinforces the fact that the distribution of power often reflects that of wealth.

   Have participants vote and tabulate the results. Announce which plan is to be implemented. Carry out this plan, redistributing the wealth if necessary.

PART C: Debriefing the Activity

Note: Debriefing is an essential step in this process.

Draw on the following questions to promote a productive discussion. Be sure to devote time to a discussion of changes needed and changes undertaken.

- How did you feel about the way in which the pennies were acquired and distributed?

- Were you treated fairly?

- Did some people give pennies away? Did you give away or receive pennies? Why or why not? How did this feel?

- What determined whether or not people gave away pennies? Knowing what the pennies represented? Having one's name displayed? Feeling guilty? Something else?

- What aspects of this game represented how the world's wealth and power are distributed?

- What about the three participants assigned to groups? Were they fairly treated? Is what happened to them similar to what happens to people around the globe? What sorts of people? Is it just chance where we end up?

- What about the participants with mittens (and scooping shovels)? What kinds of people do the mittens (and scooping shovels) represent? What group did they end up in?

- How did the members of the different groups feel about their situation? Did the recommended plan for fair distribution reflect whether the group had more or fewer pennies?

- After playing this game do you have a better understanding of the situation or attitude of poor people/nations? Of the situation or attitude of wealthy people/nations?

- Why were some people given more votes than others? Was this an accurate representation of those with more or less power in the world?

- Who are the "haves" and the "have nots" in the world today? Which countries are the "haves" and the "have nots"? Who are the "haves" and "have nots" in our country today? In our state or community? Why?

- Should the "haves" be concerned about the situation of the "have nots?" For what reasons? economic? moral/religious? political? Why might the "haves" give money or resources to the "have nots"? Is this a way to solve the problems of poverty?

- What might the "have-nots" do to improve their situation? What are some actions that "have-nots" have taken around the globe and at home to address the inequalities of wealth and power?

- Do you think there should be a redistribution of wealth and power throughout the world? Why or why not? If yes, how would you propose to accomplish this? What principles would guide your proposals for change?

- Do you think there should be a redistribution of wealth and power in this country? Why or why not? If yes, how would you propose to accomplish this? What principles would guide your proposals for change?

GOING FURTHER

1. **Media.** Ask participants to find magazine and newspaper articles about the global and/or national distribution of goods and resources and of wealth and poverty.

2. **Research.**

   a. Ask participants to find data about the distribution of wealth in the world, in the USA, and in their state or community. Have them create charts and diagrams to illustrate the distribution of wealth. Then ask them to generate questions that emerge for them from these data.

   b. Ask participants to research and write an essay on how the inequalities of distribution relate to another current issue (e.g., AIDS, health in general, the space program, crime, and environmental destruction).

3. **Films.** Show films about this topic. (See the Appendix for suggested titles.)

4. **Writing.** Immediately after debriefing the activity, ask participants to write on topics like these:

   - How do wealth and power affect one's ability to enjoy human rights and human dignity?
   - Can poor people really achieve human rights?
   - Describe how you felt about the relative position you achieved in the activity?
   - Are there responsibilities associated with having wealth and power?

ADAPTATIONS FOR YOUNGER CHILDREN

1. Younger children may need more concrete items to work for. Instead of using pennies to represent another reward, try using shelled peanuts or small wrapped candies, and tell children that they will be allowed to eat the treats when the activity has been completed. The rewards attached should be designed to be meaningful to the participants playing the game. For example, each penny could signify a certain amount of extra recess or free time in class or a special treat from the teacher. Design the rewards to be valuable enough to make authentic distinctions between the "wealthy and powerful" and the "poor and weak."

2. When debriefing with young children, focus on their views of "fair" and "unfair" and their proposals for making matters more fair. The discussion questions need to be modified for the appropriate developmental level.

Source: Written by Sherry Kempf and David Shiman, Center for World Education, University of Vermont. Adapted from S. Lamy, et al, *Teaching Global Awareness with Simulations and Games,* (Denver: Center for Teaching International Relations, University of Denver, 1994).

ACTIVITY 3

WAGES, EARNING POWER, PROFIT, AND RESPONSIBILITY: INTERNATIONAL LESSONS

OVERVIEW

The interrelated activities that comprise this lesson incorporate social studies, English, geography, and math. They help participants make connections between their own clothes and the people who make them. They pose questions about our responsibilities and suggest research-based action projects.

In Part I a brief, interactive activity identifies where participants' clothes were made and leads to an examination in Part II of the thousands of Latin American children who harvest crops in the fields or manufacture apparel in factories for export.

Time:	Part A: Where Did You Get Those Shoes (30 minutes)
	Part B: Global Marketplace on Your Back (1 hour minimum)
	Part C: Effects of Higher Wages (45 minutes)
	Part D: Work, Buying Power, and Basic Necessities (30 minutes, plus homework)
	Part E: Are My Hands Clean? (45 minutes)
	Part F: Taking Action (variable)
Materials:	• Chart paper or blackboard, markers or chalk
	• Handout 1a, *Central American Free Trade Zone Exploits Girls* and/or Handout 1b, *Kids in the Fields* or video entitled *Zoned for Slavery* (See resource list, pp. 103-105)
	• Handout 2, *Hire Rosa for 57 Cents an Hour*
	• Handout 3, *T-Shirt Math*
	• Handout 4, *Work and Basic Necessities: A Family Budget*
	• Handout 5, *Are My Hands Clean?*
	• Optional: Recording of "Are My Hands Clean?"
Setting:	Middle school – Adult groups

Sources: Part A is adapted from Mertus, Dutt, and Flowers, *Local Action/Global Change: Learning about the Human Rights of Women and Girls* (New York: UNIFEM, 1999). Parts B through E are adapted from Sanders and Sommers, *Child Labor is NOT Cheap*, (Minneapolis Resource Center of the Americas, 1997).

PART A: Where Did You Get Those Shoes? (30 minutes)

1. Ask for approximately 10 volunteers, with an even number of females and males, to come to the front of the room.

2. Ask half of the volunteers to check the labels they can find on all their clothing. The second group of volunteers will help to read the labels and call out the countries where the clothes are made. The facilitator or a volunteer makes a list of all the countries named under the heading "WHERE." Make a check for each multiple reference. Include shoes, eyeglasses, and headgear. **Note:** This works well as a homework assignment in which participants survey their closet and drawers and record information about labels and countries where apparel are made.

3. Once this list is completed, ask participants to analyze the results. In almost every case, the majority of the garments will indicate that they were made outside the USA.

   Discuss:

   • Why do you think a small group of randomly picked people in the United States is found to be wearing clothing from such diverse countries?

   • Were the brand names those of US companies? Why do US clothing companies make their products abroad?

   • Who do you think made the fabric in your clothes? Made the buttons, zippers, and other decorations? Sewed the buttonholes, set in the collar and sleeves? Was it more likely to have been a male or a female worker? An adult or a child? List these ideas under the heading "WHO." How much do you imagine that the workers who made these clothes were paid? How much should they have been paid? For example, should the workers have received pay that equals a quarter of the garment's retail price? Half? List participants' ideas on the board under the heading "THEIR PAY."

4. Ask participants what they have been paid as an hourly wage? List the wages and type of work on the board under the heading "YOUR PAY." Ask them what the minimum wage is in this country and add this amount to the list.

PART B: The Global Marketplace on Your Back (1 hour minimum)

1. Explain that this activity will link their clothes to the people who made them and the global economy.

2. Define these terms for the group and ask them to supply examples:

   CHILD LABOR: Work performed by children, often under hazardous or exploitative conditions. This does not include all work done by kids—children everywhere, for example, do chores to help their families. The 1989 UN Convention on the Rights of the Child calls for protection "against economic exploitation and against carrying out any job that might endanger well-being or educational opportunities, or that might be harmful to health or physical, mental, spiritual, moral, or social development" (Article 32).

   MAQUILADORA: A factory, often foreign-owned, that assembles goods for export. From Spanish, the word is pronounced mah-kee-lah-DOH-rah. It is usually shortened to maquila (mah-KEE-lah).

   FREE-TRADE ZONE: An industrial area in which a country allows foreign companies to import material for production and export finished goods without paying significant taxes or duties (fees to the government). A free-trade zone thus decreases a company's production costs.

3. Pass out Handout 1a, *"Central American Free Trade Zone Exploits Girls"* and/or Handout 1b, *"Kids in the Fields"* or show video entitled *Zoned for Slavery.*

   After reading or viewing, discuss:

   • What is the predominant age and gender of the workers? Why?

   • Which working conditions do you think are exploitative or demeaning?

   • How do the managers treat the workers?

   • Do the workers have opportunities to go to school?

   • Why do you think these people are willing to work for these low wages?

   • Generate adjectives to describe the workers' world?

   • Would you trade places with them?

Note: Reliable reports published in 1998 and 1999 indicate that conditions have not changed substantially in these types of worksites around the world.

4. Display on an overhead projector or pass out copies of Handout 2, *Hire Rosa for 57 Cents an Hour.* Ask participants for their reactions. Have them "free write" for five minutes. Refer to their responses in Part A about their own hourly wages.

PART C: The Effects of Higher Wages (45 minutes)

1. Introduce this math problem that evaluates a claim often made by clothing retailers when approached about requiring better wages for the workers who make our clothes. They often assert that wages must be held low so that US consumers can have inexpensive products. With some facts and some math, evaluate the validity of this claim.

2. Distribute Handout 3, *T-Shirt Math*, and provide a few minutes for participants to complete the handout individually or in pairs.

   a. Would you be willing to pay more for a shirt if that meant that workers in another country were getting higher wages? How much more? Do you think most people in the United States would be willing to do so? Why or why not?

   b. Based on only the information in this exercise, are any human rights in the Universal Declaration of Human Rights being violated? Cite specific articles.

   c. The clothing manufacturer sells its goods in the United States yet manufactures them in El Salvador. Why do you think this is the case?

   d. Who should be responsible for seeing that Salvadoran workers make wages sufficient to support themselves and their families?

PART D: Work, Buying Power, and Basic Necessities: Here and There
(30 minutes, plus homework)

1. Display on an overhead projector or pass out copies of Handout 4, *Work and Basic Necessities*. Review with participants the number of hours a Mexican must work to buy basic household items. Discuss:

   • What conclusions can they draw from the evidence of these figures?

   • What kind of life would a worker earning this wage be likely to have?

   • How do you think this low wage affects the health, leisure activities, quality of life, and planning for the future of the worker and his/her family?

2. Complete the chart at the bottom of Handout 4, *Work and Basic Necessities* by finding prices of the same goods at a local grocery store.

3. Organize research teams which will find out about child labor and working conditions in particular countries, industries, and regions of the world. Be sure they review the definition of child labor presented earlier. Have them select countries and companies based on the labels of clothes in the initial activity. (See *Organizations Working for Economic and Social Justice,* p. 106.) Participants should gather data based on the following research questions:

SCOPE OF THE PROBLEM

- Does child labor exist?
- How many child laborers?
- Which industries employ child laborers?
- Why do the children work?

WORK CONDITIONS

- How are the children treated?
- How much are they paid?
- What hazards and risks do they face?

CONTRIBUTING FACTORS

- Why do the countries (or countries in the region) allow child labor?
- Why do companies hire child labor even when it's illegal? Are the reasons economic? political? social?
- How do children become laborers? What are their family and socio-economic conditions?

RESPONSES

- What do international documents (e.g., Convention on the Rights of the Child, Universal Declaration of Human Rights) say about child labor?
- What do international organizations (e.g., United Nations, International Labor Organization) do to halt child labor?
- What does your government do to halt child labor?
- Who is working on the solution?
- What are they doing?

PART E: Are My Hands Clean? (45 minutes)

1. Play or read the song on Handout 5, *Are My Hands Clean* (Recorded by Sweet Honey in the Rock in the album *Still on the Journey*)

Discuss:

• How many countries are mentioned in the song?

• How many corporations are mentioned and why are they located in different parts of the world?

• Why does the making of the blouse require so much transportation between the industrial world and the "third" or developing world?

• What human rights issues are raised in the song?

• Do you think it is fair to suggest that those who buy these products have "dirty hands"? If not, how would you describe these purchasers? Does this description fit you? If so, are you comfortable with it? If not, what might you do about it?

• What would it take for people to have "clean hands"?

• Given the widespread problem of child labor and abuse, how can one become a more socially conscious shopper?

• How can we help others become more conscious of their participation in this "dirty business"?

PART F: Taking Action (Variable)

There are numerous opportunities for informed, value-based action. Below are some approaches, including contacting web sites, monitoring and affecting personal and institutional purchasing practices, and influencing international companies and local stores.

1. Have the group discuss the Ladder of Labor Responsibility (below) developed by Co-op America (See p. 29). It is a new tool for consumers to determine the labor conditions behind the products they buy. As of 1999, they have developed ladders for athletic shoes, tea, coffee, hand-knotted Oriental carpets, and blue jeans.

The Ladder of Labor Responsibility

a) *Top Rung* companies are green businesses and fair-trade organizations that are models of how business can be done to respect people and the planet. These companies sprang up as alternatives to business as usual.

b) *Upper Rung* companies have codes of conduct that are being independently monitored and enforced, pay a living wage, and are also engaged in development work in the communities where their workers live.

c) *Lower and Middle Rung* companies have corporate codes of conduct to protect workers, but may or may not be enforcing them. Some have enforced codes of conduct, but do not pay their workers a living wage that provides for basic needs.

d) *Bottom Rung* companies have not yet adopted a code of conduct or started to monitor and enforce the practices of their suppliers and subcontractors. Bottom rung companies might also be flagrantly violating their own codes of conduct.

2. As a group, identify those sporting goods and clothing apparel that your school district or recreation department purchases (e.g. balls, t-shirts, uniforms, sports shoes, and band uniforms) or relevant purchases made by the fire and police departments and janitorial services. Conduct research into the labor practices (wages, conditions of employment) of the companies that manufacture these products. Based on findings, have participants develop a plan to promote fair, humane purchasing practices by the school and municipality.

3. Ask participants to consider the personal actions to end sweatshops suggested below. Discuss the pros and cons of each of these. Have participants role play these actions to help them become more effective agents of change.

- Choose one product that you buy often (coffee, gifts, clothing) and purchase it only from a green business or a fair-trade organization.

- Raise awareness. Ask one retail store each month if its products were manufactured without exploiting anyone and how they know.

- Write, call, or e-mail one manufacturer each month from which you regularly make purchases. Ask them where they are on the Ladder of Labor Responsibility and urge them to take the next step. Be sure to note how frequently you purchase their products. Request a reply.

- Select an action campaign and become involved. (See addresses below.)

- Whenever possible, buy products that you know are produced by companies that enforce fair labor practices and respect the Earth. Buy from community-based businesses.

- Remember to monitor investments. Make sure your (or your parents') financial planner is screening for labor issues.

Source: Adapted from <www.sweatshops.org>, *Five Simple Steps to End Sweatshops.*

4. Resources, Campaigns, and Companies

   a. Books, Government Publications, Educational Guides

By Sweat and Toil of Children, Department of Labor, Bureau of International Labor Affairs, Child Labor Division, Room S-5202, Washington, DC 20210, Tel: (202) 208-4843, <www.dol.gov/dol/iab/publicmediareports/childnew.htm>.

Child Labor is NOT Cheap, a three-lesson curriculum for youths through adults, Resource Center for the Americas, 317-17th Ave SE, Minneapolis, MN 55314-2077, Tel: (612) 627-0445.

Consumers' Guide to Fairly Traded Products, Fair Trade Federation, P.O. Box 126. Barre, MA 01005, Tel: (508) 355-0284.

Global Sweatshop Curriculum Packet for 4th through 12th graders, Campaign for Labor Rights, 1247 E. Street SE, Washington, DC 20003, Tel: (541) 344-5410.

Made in China: Behind the Label, National Labor Committee, 275 7th Avenue, New York, NY 10001, Tel: (212) 242-3002, <www.nlcet.org>.

The Department of Labor's Employment Standards Agency, Wage and Hour Division, 200 Constitution Ave. NW, Washington, DC 20210, Tel: (212) 693-0051, <www.dol.gov/dol/esa>.

Shopping for a Better World, Council on Economic Priorities, 30 Irving Place, New York, NY 10003, Tel: (212) 420-1133, <www.realaudio.com/CEP/home.html>.

   b. Campaigns for Fair Labor Practices

Campaign for Labor Rights, 1247 E Street SE, Washington, DC 20003, Tel: (541) 344-5410, <www.summersault.com/~agj/clr>. Publishes newsletter with up-to-date information on all sweatshop campaigns and analysis of current labor-rights issues.

Co-op America, 1612 K St. NW, #600, Washington, DC 20006, Tel: (202) 872-5307, <www.coopamerica.org>. Conducts anti-sweatshop campaigns targeting Disney, publishes National Green Pages, <www.greenpages.org>, and sponsors <www.sweatshops.org>.

Fair Trade Federation, P.O. Box 126, Barre, MA 01005, Tel: (508) 355-0284, <www.fairtradefederation.com>. Promotes fair-trade products and businesses.

National Labor Committee, 275 7th Avenue, 15th Fl., New York, NY 10001, Tel: (212) 242-3002, <www.nlcnet.org>. Coordinates Disney, Wal-Mart, K-mart, and many other campaigns.

Sweatshop Watch, 310 8th St., Ste. 309, Oakland, CA 94607, Tel: (510) 834-8990, <www.sweatshopwatch.org>. A coalition of organizations committed to eliminating sweatshops.

c. Some Companies to Contact

Disney
500 S. Buena Vista St.
Burbank, CA 91521
818-846-7319 (FAX)

Esprit
900 Minnesota St.
San Francisco, CA 94107

GAP INC.
1 Harrison St.
San Francisco, CA 94105
415-952-4400
415-495-2922 (fax)

Guess?
1444 S. Alameda St.
Los Angeles, CA 90021

J.C. Penney
100 Commercial Rd.
Leominster, MA 01453

K-Mart
3100 W. Big Beaver Rd.
Troy, MI 48084

Nike
One Bowerman Dr.
Beaverton, OR 97005-6453

WalMart
702 SW Eighth St.
Bentonville, AR 72716-8611

Victoria's Secret/Intimate Brands, Inc.
3 Limited Pkwy.
Columbus, OH 43230

May Company
611 Olive St.
St. Louis, MO 63101

Central American Free Trade Zones Exploit Girls

(excerpted from *The New York Times*, July 26, 1995)

by Bob Herbert

The next time you pick up a safari jacket at Banana Republic, or a pair of jeans at the Gap, or an Eddie Bauer T-shirt, give a moment's thought to girls like Claudia Molina and Judith Viera, teen-agers who have had to work under extremely cruel conditions to produce much of that clothing.

Until recently, Ms. Molina and Ms. Viera were maquiladora workers - young people employed by the hundreds of thousands in free-trade-zone factories in Central America and the Caribbean to make goods for the US market.

The US companies that benefit from the near-enslavement of these workers pretend not to know about the abuses in the factories, which are independently owned.

Ms. Molina's last employer was Orion Apparel, a Korean-owned plant in Honduras that produces, among other items, shirts for Gitano, a subsidiary of Fruit of the Loom. Ms. Molina was paid 38 cents an hour in a sweatshop that employed girls as young as 14.

The work schedule at Orion could have been fashioned in the Dark Ages. When business is especially good--that is, when the big orders from the US companies roll in--the Monday-through-Friday schedule is 7:30 a.m. to 10:30 p.m., a 15-hour shift. Saturday is the long day. The workers go in at 7:30 a.m. and don't re-emerge until Sunday at 6 a.m.--a 22-hour shift!

Charles Kemaghan, executive director of the National Labor Committee in New York, which is fighting the exploitation of maquiladora workers, said there was nothing unusual about the work schedule at Orion.

"It's a race to the bottom," he said. "The idea is to find those workers who will accept the lowest wages, the fewest benefits and the most miserable working conditions."

The vast majority of the maquiladora workers are poverty-stricken girls and young women. (Ms. Molina, for example, lives with four relatives in a one-room shack with no running water.)

The companies make no secret of their preference for young females. A common explanation is that girls at about the age of 16 are at their peak of hand and eye coordination, perfect for the factories. A more persuasive explanation is that young girls are the most docile of all workers, less likely to object to abuse or to fight for any rights.

Because so many of the workers are so young, the scene outside the factories each morning can resemble a schoolyard. Some of the workers are actually driven to the plants in traditional yellow school buses.

Once inside, the youngsters are worked like demons. Talking is forbidden. Bathroom visits are limited to two a day. Requests for medical attention are discouraged.

Many of the workers would like to go to school in the evenings, but the bosses won't let them. The youngsters would have to leave the plant too early to get to class on time.

Judith Viera was part of an effort to form a union at Mandarin International, a Taiwanese-owned plant in El Salvador that makes clothing for the Gap, Eddie Bauer and others.

Back in February Ms. Viera and her co-workers succeeded in establishing the first union ever to be legally recognized in a free-trade zone in El Salvador. It wasn't much of a triumph.

The union is now all but broken. Ms. Viera and her two sisters were among some 350 union members who were illegally fired by Mandarin. She was making 56 cents an hour when she lost her job.

The free-trade zones, promoted by the Reagan and Bush administrations and financed to a great extent by US tax dollars, have been a bonanza for US companies, but the human toll they are taking is unconscionable.

Since 1980, the US has lost more than half a million textile and apparel jobs. Meanwhile, the wages paid to the maquiladora workers are so low they will not even cover the food necessary to satisfy minimal nutrition requirements.

Claudia Molina and Judith Viera have been brought to the United States by the National Labor Committee to tell their story. How long can we, like the big apparel companies, refuse to hear them?

All that is joyful in life is being wrung from the youngsters who are fed into the wretched, soulless system of the maquiladora assembly plants.

Is a Gap shirt worth it?

Kids in the Fields

by David Bacon
Mexicali Valley, Baja California, Mexico

From a distance, the green-onion field looks almost festive. Strung between pieces of iron rods, dozens of colored cloth sheets ripple in the morning breeze and shelter workers from the Mexicali Valley sun. The soft conversation of hundreds of people, sitting in rows next to great piles of green onions, fills the air. The vegetable's pungent scent is everywhere. Wandering among the workers are toddlers, some nursing on baby bottles and others chewing on the onions. A few sleep in the rows, and some in vegetable bins in makeshift beds of blankets.

But the toddlers aren't the only children in this field. Dozens of the workers, perhaps a quarter, range in age from 6 to 16. The foreman, who doesn't reveal his name, says it's normal for his 300-person crew to include entire families, youngsters and all. The workers, he says, are employed by the Oxnard, California-based Muranaka Farms.

The children are some of the hidden victims of the North American Free Trade Agreement, a controversial deal between the United States, Mexico and Canada. Since NAFTA took effect in 1994, US growers such as Muranaka have relocated production across the border. Their profiteering, subsidized by the Mexican government, intensified an economic crisis marked by the December 1994 plunge in the value of Mexican currency. As the incomes of poor Mexicans dropped by almost half, desperation pushed new waves of children into the fields. Thousands of kids now produce crops destined for dinner tables in northern cities around the world, from Minneapolis to Tokyo.

Targeting these markets, joint ventures between Mexican and US growers "are achieving greater competitiveness at the cost of children working in the fields," says Gema López Limón, an education professor at the Autonomous University of Baja California, who investigates child labor in agriculture. "We're creating a workforce without education, condemned to the lowest wages and to periods of great unemployment."

ACQUIESCENCE: Like the United States, Mexico outlaws child labor. Article 123 of the nation's constitution says children under 14 may not work, and those between 14 and 16 may work only six hours a day. Article 22 of the federal labor law likewise bars employment under 14, and permits work between 14 and 16 only by special permission and only if the children have completed an elementary education.

While government statistics do not track the number of working children, Mexico's Labor and Social Forecasting Secretariat estimates that various economic sectors employ a total of 800,000 workers under 14. Based on the 1990 census, the Public Education Secretariat guesses that more than 2.5 million kids between 6 and 14 don't attend school.

The second International Independent Tribunal Against Child Labor, held in Mexico City in March 1996, concluded that the economic forces behind expanded Mexican child labor were having the same effect in other countries. The number of working children globally has climbed to more than 250 million, according to the International Labor Organization (ILO). "Trade agreements like NAFTA and [the General Agreement on Tariffs and Trade] promised protections for workers," López testified. "But they don't prohibit child labor, they regulate it."

After three days of testimony by witnesses from 18 countries, the tribunal called for ratifying the 1973 ILO Convention 138, which bans labor by school-age children. Only 58 countries had signed the pact, and neither Mexico nor the United States had ratified it. María Estela Ríos González, president of the Mexican National Association of Democratic Lawyers, says international support for the convention buckled under big-business pressure.

To upstage the ILO blanket ban on child labor, the United Nations formulated another convention, Number 32, in 1989. This one, while decrying child labor, allows each nation to determine an age at which children may work and to regulate the circumstances of their labor. Mexico and many other countries that refuse to ratify the ILO measure have adopted the UN approach. Free-market champions have rallied behind the UN convention because they hope regulating child labor will undermine efforts to eliminate it.

"We cannot substitute the labor of countless children for the inadequate income of their parents," Ríos González says. "During all the history of humanity, adults have been the protectors and nurturers of children. Now children are nurturing and protecting the adults. We are robbing them of their future."

DROP-OUTS: María, 12, works along-side her mother in the Muranaka field. "My grandmother told me this year that we didn't have enough money for me to go to school," she says. "At first I stayed home to take care of my little sister, but it was boring, and sometimes it was scary being by ourselves all day. So I came to work here. We need the money."

Honorina Ruiz, 6, sits nearby in front of a green-onion pile. She lines up eight or nine onions, straightening out their roots and tails. Then she knocks off the dirt, puts a rubber band around them, and adds the bunch to a box beside her. Too shy to say more than her name, she seems proud to be able to do what her brother Rigoberto, at 13, has become very good at.

Some 3,000 children work in Mexicali Valley's green-onion harvest, says López, the education professor. The October-June growing season, which coincides with the academic year, hurts school attendance. While the valley's population has increased in recent years--the city of Mexicali alone boasts more than 600,000 inhabitants--rural schools keep losing children.

At the Alfredo A. Uchurtu primary school in the heart of the green-onion district, teacher Pedro González Hernández says 40 of 252 enrollees had dropped out by the end of the 1995-1996 season. Attendance began to fall in 1987, when the school had 363 kids. "That's the year we had the first economic collapse in Mexico," he recalls.

"Not only can't they come, but often they don't want to." González admits. "With all the problems they've had in keeping up, when they do come, they face blame."

"We've tried to devise a kind of study that these children can do at home," he adds. "It will never be as good as attending class, but at least it's some alternative."

In another effort, Baja California teachers have convinced the state government to offer $15.73 a month and food coupons to rural children who would otherwise have to work. Twenty-five kids at Uchurtu get the allowance, and all of them are still in class. But the program lacks funds to help all the kids who need it, and some government officials are rumored to have diverted allowances for their own children.

Even with more funds and proper administration, such measures would likely fall short in the NAFTA era. "What drives children into the fields is that the wages their parents receive isn't enough to support the family," González says.

In 1996, Mexicali Valley companies paid about $.11 for a dozen bunches of onions. For an adult, a good day's work amounted to $6.66. A young child, on the other hand, would produce enough to earn only about $3. Field workers said the growers hadn't raised the piece rate since 1995, despite grocery price hikes. In 1996, a gallon of milk rose from $2 to $2.33, more than a third of an adult's daily wages.

Adults and children work the same day, usually from 5:30 a.m. to 4 p.m. There is no overtime pay, except for work on Sunday. The Muranaka field had just one portable bathroom for the whole crew. A metal drum on wheels held drinking water. The climate adds to the misery. Mexicali Valley, extending south from the border of California and Arizona, is an irrigated desert. In late spring, despite the cloth shelters, it gets brutally hot. In winter, the temperature can drop to freezing.

FLIGHT: Muranaka is among numerous US vegetable producers that operate in Mexico. Besides the green onions, the produce includes spinach, radishes, cilantro, parsley, kale, leeks and beets--all processed in Mexicali Valley packing sheds.

Carisa Wright of Muranaka Farms says her firm considers its Mexican operations profitable, and is expanding them. "Most of our operations are labor intensive, so we do save money on labor costs by comparison with those in the US," she notes.

Muranaka management would not answer specific questions about its use of children. "As far as we know," a company letter states, "our growers comply in the fullest with Mexican federal and state labor laws to the best of their abilities." Workers, the letter adds, "are over the minimum legal working age."

Tom Nunes of the Nunes Company, a large vegetable grower based in Salinas, California, contracts with a Mexicali Valley grower. The grower cultivates the onions, packs them in ice, and sends them to Nunes. Nunes sells the onions at market prices, then gives the grower what's left after deducting for seeds, cartons, loading, customs duties, and a sales charge. Nunes estimates he profits only $.01 per bunch.

Could the company sell the bunch for an extra penny to raise field-worker wages? "There's no incentive for us to do that," Nunes responds. "There are no green onions grown now in the US in the winter, because they can't compete with the price of those grown in Mexico."

"I wouldn't go over there if this competition didn't exit," he says. "The power of the market is stronger than all of us."

Calling it a free market, however, would be a mistake. To lure US investment, the Mexican government promises a low-wage workforce and a wealth of subsidies. Direct assistance starts with irrigated water, which is much cheaper in Mexicali Valley than across the border in California's Imperial Valley.

"What we need is to produce food, first, for people to eat here in Mexico, where people are actually hungry and where no one buys these green onions," says López, the education professor. "Then, if we have extra capacity to produce, we can sell the rest on the market in the US or anywhere else. The government makes the same kind of argument about the maquiladoras (export-oriented assembly plants)—that they bring jobs. Yes, but are they jobs with a future that a family can live on?"

Source: A. Sanders and M. Sommers, *Child Labor is Not Cheap*
(Minneapolis: Resource Center of the Americas, 1997).

HIRE ROSA FOR 57¢ AN HOUR

by David Bacon
Mexicali Valley, Baja California, Mexico

'Hire Rosa for 57 Cents an Hour!'

This advertisement appeared in the August 1990 edition of *Bobbin,* a trade magazine of the U.S. garment industry. When the ad appeared a year later, it had been changed to, "You can hire Rosa Martinez for *33 cents* an hour." (Emphasis added.)

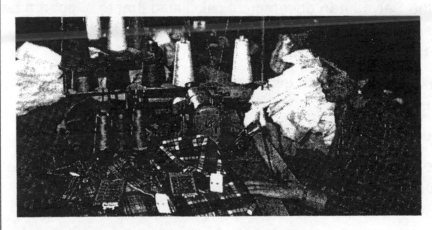

Quality, Industriousness and Reliability Is What El Salvador Offers You!

Rosa Martinez produces apparel for U.S. markets on her sewing machine in El Salvador. You can hire her for 57 cents an hour*.

Rosa is more than just colorful. She and her co-workers are known for their industriousness, reliability and quick learning. They make El Salvador one of the best buys in the C.B.I. In addition, El Salvador has excellent road and sea transportation (including Central America's most modern airport) . . . **and** there are **no** quotas.

Find out more about **sourcing** in El Salvador. Contact **FUSADES**, the private, non-profit and non-partisan organization promoting social and economic development in El Salvador. Miami telephone: 305/381-8940.

* - Does not include fringe benefits.

Source: A. Sanders and M. Sommers, *Child Labor is Not Cheap* (Minneapolis: Resource Center of the Americas, 1997).

T-SHIRT MATH

Take, for example, a t-shirt that sells for $20.00 in the United States. This shirt is manufactured by an international corporation at one of its factories in El Salvador. This factory is one example of a *maquiladora,* which is a foreign-owned factory that assembles goods for export.

The Salvadoran workers producing the shirt were paid $ .56 an hour.
On average, a worker is able to sew approximately 4.7 shirts per hour.

Using the information above, calculate the following:

• How much does a worker receive per t-shirt?_____

In 1994, the Salvadoran government calculated that to support a family at a bare-subsistence level, it would take approximately four times the wages provided by maquiladora worker.

• If a worker's wages were quadrupled, how much would they make
  per hour?_____

• How much would they earn per t-shirt?_____

• If the company passed on this increased cost to the consumer,
  how much would a t-shirt cost?

Now imagine that a worker's wages were increased by ten times.

• What would be their hourly rate?_____

• How much would they earn per shirt?_____

• If the company passed on this increased cost to the consumer,
  how much would you pay for the t-shirt?_____

Source: A. Sanders and M. Sommers, *Child Labor is Not Cheap*
(Minneapolis: Resource Center of the Americas, 1997).

WORK AND BASIC NECESSITIES: A FAMILY BUDGET

A typical worker in Mexico earns about 26 pesos ($3.60) a day. This chart shows how many paid hours it takes to buy a few basic necessities. The figures reflect average prices in Tijuana, the city across the border from San Diego. A kilogram is 2.2 pounds.

Necessity	Hours of Work
Beans, 1 kilogram	4 hours
Rice, 1 kilogram	1 hour, 26 minutes
Tomatoes, 1 kilogram	1 hour, 35 minutes
Beef, 1 kilogram	8 hours
Chicken, 1 kilogram	3 hours
Egg, 1 dozen	2 hours, 24 minutes
Milk, 1 gallon	4 hours, 17 minutes
Toilet paper, 1 roll	43 minutes
Diapers, a box of 30	11 hours, 30 minutes
Shampoo, 10 ounces	2 hours, 25 minutes
School uniform (mandatory)	57-86 hours
One school book	17-20 hours
Aspirin, a bottle of 20	2 hours, 25 minutes

Activity: Go to a grocery store and check the prices of the same items. Then calculate how many hours of work, at your wage, it would take for you to buy them (a kilogram equals 2.2 pounds). **Note:** Some participants might compare the prices in rich and poor parts of their town to get different view of the buying power of income.

Your wage: _____ / hour

Necessity	Grocery Store Price	Hours of Work at Your Wage
Beans, 1 kilogram	_____	_____
Rice, 1 kilogram	_____	_____
Tomatoes, 1 kilogram	_____	_____
Beef, 1 kilogram	_____	_____
Chicken, 1 kilogram	_____	_____
Egg, 1 dozen	_____	_____
Milk, 1 gallon	_____	_____
Toilet paper, 1 roll	_____	_____
Diapers, a box of 30	_____	_____
Shampoo, 10 ounces	_____	_____
School uniform (mandatory)	_____	_____
One school book	_____	_____
Aspirin, a bottle of 20	_____	_____

Source: A. Sanders and M. Sommers, *Child Labor is Not Cheap*
(Minneapolis: Resource Center of the Americas, 1997).

ARE MY HANDS CLEAN?

I wear garments touched by hands from all over the world
35% cotton, 6% polyester, the journey begins in Central America
In the cotton fields of El Salvador
In a province soaked in blood,
Pesticide-sprayed workers toil in a broiling sun
Pulling cotton for two dollars a day.

Then we move on up to another rung - Cargill
A top-forty trading conglomerate, takes the cotton through the Panama Canal
Up the Eastern seaboard, coming to the US of A for the first time

In South Carolina
At the Burlington mils
Joins a shipment of polyester filament courtesy of the
New Jersey petro-chemical mills of Dupont

Dupont strands of filament begin in the South American country of Venezuela
Where oil riggers bring up oil from the earth for six dollars a day
Then Exxon, largest oil company in the world,
Upgrades the product in the country of Trinidad and Tobago
Then back into the Caribbean and Atlantic Seas
To the factories of Dupont
On the way to the Burlington mills
In South Carolina
To meet the cotton from the blood-soaked fields of El Salvador

In South Carolina
Burlington factories hum with the business of weaving oil and cotton into miles of fabric of Sears
Who takes this bounty back into the Caribbean Sea
Headed for Haiti this time -
May she be one day soon free -
Far from the Port-au-Prince palace
Third world women toil doing piece work to Sears specifications
For three dollars a day my sisters make my blouse
It leaves the third world for the last time
Coming back into the sea to be sealed in plastic for me
This third world sister
And I go to the Sears department store where I buy my blouse
On sale for 20% discount

Are my hands clean?

(Song composed for Winterfest, Institute for Policy Studies. The lyrics are based on an article by Institute
fellow John Cavanaugh, "The Journey of the Blouse: A Global Assembly." Lyrics and music by Bernice
Johnson Reagon. Songtalk Publishing Co. 1985)

ACTIVITY 4

COMMUNITY RESEARCH AND ACTION PLAN: ECONOMIC AND SOCIAL RIGHTS

OVERVIEW

This activity enables participants to become knowledgeable about selected local and global human rights conditions. They research human rights problems in their community, analyze and report on data gathered, and develop an action plan to address problems related to social and economic rights. Although built around the issues of homelessness, hunger, lack of adequate health care, and inadequate employment wages and conditions, this format is adaptable to other human rights concerns.

Time: Variable

Materials: Copies of Universal Declaration of Human Rights (UDHR)

Optional (for national/global data gathering): US Department of Commerce, Bureau of the Census, *Statistical Abstract of the United States* (yearly). United Nations Development Programme, *Human Development Report*, NY: Oxford University Press, (yearly). World Bank, *World Development Report*, NY: Oxford University Press, (yearly). Reddy, Marlita A. (ed). *Statistical Abstract of the World*, New York: Gale Research, 1994. UNICEF, *The State of the World's Children* (yearly). local community directories, telephone books.

Setting: Middle school – Adult groups

PROCEDURE

Note: You might introduce this activity in a least three different ways depending on your goals, the time available, and/or the participants: 1) presenting the concept of social, economic, and cultural rights, as found in Articles 22-27 of the UDHR and then have the group try to identify rights problems in their community for each Article; 2) collecting newspaper articles or brainstorming about problems in the community and then moving to making links with social, economic, and cultural rights found in the UDHR; 3) identifying (alone or with a planning group) a few local problems and using them to frame the initial discussion and subsequent activity. This activity illustrates this third approach.

1. **Read/Discuss:**

Read the following quotation by Eleanor Roosevelt, Chair of the UN Human Rights Commission which created the UDHR, to participants:

> Where, after all, do universal rights begin? In places, close to home—so close and so small that cannot be seen on any maps of the world. Yet they are the world of the individual person; the neighborhood he lives in; the school or college he attends; the factory, farm, or office where he works. Such are the places where every man, woman and child seeks equal justice, equal opportunity, equal dignity without discrimination. Unless these right have meaning there, they have little meaning anywhere. Without concerted citizen action to uphold them close to home, we shall look in vain for progress in the large world.

Eleanor Roosevelt, *The Great Question* (NY: United Nations, 1958).

2. **Brainstorm:**

Write the four problem areas (e.g., homelessness, hunger, lack of adequate health care, inadequate employment wages and conditions) on a chalkboard or chart paper. Discuss the following questions, recording responses as declarative sentences, (e.g. "People are homeless.")

- Do the problems exist in our community? Are they severe? What are our sources of information? Are they reliable and complete?

- From what individuals, groups, or organizations can we get informed data about the problem in our community?

- Are there other more pressing concerns that we should study rather than those suggested above?

3. **Discuss:**

Introduce the UDHR and indicate how this activity relates to this document. In particular, call the group's attention to Articles 22-27 in the UDHR. Have them identify those articles that refer to the issues being discussed, and, if time permits, have them read the relevant articles aloud. Discuss language that is unclear and identify definitional problems.

Note: For advanced groups, also introduce the International Covenant on Social, Economic and Cultural Rights. Explain briefly how it relates to the UDHR (e.g., the UDHR is a statement of principles while the International Covenant is a binding agreement.)

4. **List:**

Identify individuals, organizations, or agencies that address these societal problems and work to support or promote these human rights.

Note: This might be a small group research project. These will serve as sources of information (e.g., the interviewees, for the community research effort). Consider such organizations as food shelves, legal aid, homeless shelters, meals on wheels, labor unions, tenants rights associations, and "free" community health clinics.

5. **Preparing for Research:**

Divide the participants into research teams to explore one of these human rights issues. Each team should: a) identify individuals and groups from Step 4 to interview and set up these meetings, b) plan its interview questions, drawing on those provided below and developing questions of their own, and c) assign responsibilities (e.g., who will conduct interviews, gather background information from library and web sources).

6. **Conduct Research:**

Each team then researches its human rights issue. Some will conduct interviews in their community to determine the extent of the problem and what is being done to address it. Others might gather data through library research or on the World Wide Web, thus placing the local situation in a larger societal/global context. A member of each team should visit a site in the community that addresses its human rights issue.

7. **Report Research Findings:**

Each team submits a written report and develops a presentation highlighting its findings for the rest of the group. This might involve art, video, role-play, music, or any other medium to communicate their findings and indicate what actions need to be taken to address the problem. Teams might write an article for a local or school newspaper or invite "the press" to their presentations.

8. **Plan to Act:**

After discussing their findings and weighing their action options, participants decide on a human rights problem to adopt as a project. Brainstorm ways in which they can become involved and begin to develop of plan of action. This might involve joining with activists already working on the problem selected. December 10, which is Human Rights Day, might be designated as class project decision day.

9. **Act:**

The group then carries out its plan to address the human rights problem. Activities might include educating school and community via posters, plays, street theater, school assemblies and community speakers, newspaper articles, and public demonstrations. They can also engage in letter writing campaigns, organizing public consciousness-raising concerts, lobbying government officials and elected representatives, raising funds to support local and global relief and development agencies, and volunteering services to local or international organizations.

In a school, these activities can easily be connected to the participants' academic work. Participants can accomplish this by conducting research and recording, analyzing, and sharing their experiences through class presentations and written reports. There are also many opportunities for participants to express themselves through art, video, music, and drama, and to incorporate mathematics (e.g., percentages, graphs, and proportions) into their work.

10. **Evaluate:**

The group evaluates the experience in terms of impact on them personally, effect of their efforts on improving a condition, and lessons learned about trying to make a change.

Source: Written by Karen Kraco and David Shiman, Center for World Education, University of Vermont. Adapted from *Human Rights Education: The Fourth R* (Chicago: Human Rights Educators' Network, Amnesty International USA, Spring 1998).

Common Interview Questions (For All Issues)

Describing the Problem

• What is the problem as you see it?

• How does the problem manifest itself locally? Nationally? Globally? (See suggested sources above for national/global data.)

• Do those members of the community who do not have _____ (insert appropriate theme) tend to come from particular groups (e.g., income, sections of town, age, race/ethnicity, gender, ability/disability, citizenship status, language)? Do they share any other similarities (e.g., attitude, legal status)?

• What is being done locally, nationally, and globally to address this issue? (See suggested sources above for national/global data.)

• What services exist in your community to support people denied this human right? Who provides these services (e.g., public funding, private agencies, individuals)?

• Do the services reach those in need? Have the services be expanded or curtailed in recent years? If so, to what effect?

Uncovering Associated Conditions

• What policies and practices contribute to the violation or denial of this human right?

• How are these four human rights issues (e.g., homelessness, hunger, lack of adequate health care, and inadequate employment wages and conditions) interrelated?

• Are there some who benefit and others who suffer, directly or indirectly, as a result of the situation that presently exists?

• How do people justify or explain that certain people have this basic need met (and much more!) while others do not? Do you find these explanations convincing? Explain.

• Do you consider _____(insert topic) to be a human right to which everyone is entitled?

• Do you think it is appropriate and/or fair that some in the community lack this condition and others have it?

Planning for Change

• Identify policies, practices, and/or attitudes that need to be modified, strengthened, or eliminated and new ones that need to be initiated.

• What might the participants do to help promote these human rights in their community?

Issue-Specific Interview Questions

Homelessness

- Are there homeless people in this community? How many?

- How many are served by shelters? How many are not?

- How accurate are these numbers? How are they determined?

- Have the numbers of homeless been going up or down? Explain

- Are there characteristics that many homeless people have in common? Is there a typical age? Gender? Racial or ethnic group? How do they become homeless?

- Has the composition of the homeless population been changing? Explain.

- What effect have government policies had on creating homelessness?

- What's the likelihood that those who are homeless also share other characteristics (e.g., have been deinstitutionalized, have substance abuse problem, have experienced domestic violence, have a mental or physical disability, are unemployed, and/or are under 18 years of age)?

- What permanent housing is available? What factors help them find housing?

- Is the housing adequate (e.g., number of units, conditions)? Are there people on waiting lists?

- Are conditions in this housing healthy and safe (e.g., free of rats, lead paint, structural damage, environmental pollution, electrical/fire hazards, gang/drug related violence)?

- Are services provided in a respectful way to those in need?

Hunger

- Are there people in this community who are hungry on a regular basis? Who are they?

- How accurate are these numbers? How are they determined?

- Have the number of hungry people been going up or down? Explain.

- Are there characteristics that many hungry people have in common? Is there a typical age? Gender? Racial or ethnic group?

- Has the composition of the hungry population been changing? Explain.

- Are there people who hold full-time employment but whose family are still hungry and malnourished? How is this possible?

- What factors have contributed to their lacking food?

- What services are available to help hungry people in our community?

- Who offers these services? Are they funded by the government or private institutions or agencies?

- Are services provided in a respectful way to those in need?

- Have the numbers needing food assistance increased on decrease recently? Explain.

- Have food assistance programs been expanding or contracting recently? Explain.

Lack of Adequate Health Care

- Are there people in this community who need health care but are unable to get it?

- Are there people denied health care or insurance? What do these people do when they are sick or injured?

- Are there people who receive inadequate care?

- How accurate are these numbers? How are they determined?

- Have the numbers of those with inadequate health care been going up or down? Explain.

- Are there characteristics that those lacking adequate health care have in common? Is there a typical age? Gender? Racial or ethnic group? How do they become lacking in health care?

- Has the composition of the population lacking adequate health care been changing? Explain.

- What services are available for people who cannot afford to pay for health care? Are they funded by the government or private institutions or agencies?

- What pre- and post-natal services are available for low income mothers? Are services provided in a respectful way to those in need?

- Has the number of people lacking health care and insurance increased or decreased recently?

Inadequate Employment Wages and Conditions

- How would you define a living wage?

- Are there people employed in this community who do not receive a living wage?

- Are there people forced to work in dangerous or unhealthy conditions?

- Are working conditions fair for all (male/female, black/white)?

- Is there equal pay for equal work?

- Are there people denied the right to organize at their place of work?

- Are there people denied opportunities for advancement and professional development?

- Are people forced to work to obtain public assistance benefits?

- What are the child care concerns of low wage earners? Are they being addressed? If so, how? If not, why?

ACTIVITY 5

HUNGER USA

Participants explore their attitudes and values and develop an understanding of the relationships between hunger and other poverty-related factors in the USA. In addition, they identify actions they might take. Activities can be used separately or as an integrated curriculum.

Time:	Part A: Exploring Attitudes - Voting with your Feet (45 minutes)
	Part B: Creating a Concept Web (45 minutes)
	Part C: What are the Effects of... (45 minutes)
	Part D: Family Budget Activity (45 minutes)
	Part E: Taking Action (Variable)
Materials:	• Handout 1, *Hunger & Poverty Statements*
	• Handout 2, *Family Budget Sheet*
	• Copies of Universal Declaration of Human Rights (UDHR)
Setting:	Middle school – Adult groups

PROCEDURE

Note: Keep in mind the socioeconomic composition of your participant population. Guard against having this activity confirm the existing inequalities in wealth and power or make certain participants uncomfortable.

**PART A: Exploring Attitudes about Hunger and Poverty–
Voting with your Feet (45 minutes)**

1. Create a continuum on the board or the floor by writing STRONGLY AGREE at one end and STRONGLY DISAGREE at the other. Explain to participants that you will read statements about hunger and poverty in the United States. After each statement, they are to indicate their level of agreement by "voting with their feet," walking to a spot on a continuum along the floor that reflects their opinion. Record the distribution of participant opinions on the board for the subsequent discussion. **Note:** Be sure to allow for those participants who feel uncomfortable participating in this activity.

2. Read some suggested statements and have the participants move about:

   - If people are hungry, it's probably because they are wasting their money on other things.

   - There is enough food to go around.

   - Hunger and poverty are due to laziness and lack of ambition.

   - There is no hunger in my community.

   - I don't think I will ever go hungry.

   - I would give away some of my own food or wealth to ensure that others did not go hungry.

   - People are hungry because they are poor.

   - People are poor because political and economic policies keep them poor.

   - Hunger limits people's ability to learn and be productive.

   - The presence of hunger and poverty in this country is evidence that there is something wrong with our national priorities.

   - The government should do more to help those who are poor.

   - There will always be hunger and poverty.

   - People are hungry and poor because the rich have more than their fair share.

3. Conduct a follow-up discussion built around the following questions:

   - Which statements generated the most agreement? Which were most controversial? How do you explain this?

   - On what were you basing your opinions? Where did you get your information?

   - How did you feel about openly expressing your opinions on poverty and hunger?

   - What new thoughts or questions emerged for you as a result of doing this exercise?

4. Break participants into small groups and give each group Handout 1, *Hunger and Poverty Statements*. Ask the group to read the statements aloud together and discuss these questions:

   - Were any facts on this sheet a surprise and/or new information to you?

   - Do any of these facts change the way you "voted with your feet" at the start of the activity?

5. Bring the whole group back together and ask each group to report on their responses to the questions in Step 4 above. List any statements that might have caused them to "vote" differently.

6. Choose two or three of these statements and repeat Step 2. Record changes in positions on the original chart.

7. Conclude the activity with a brief discussion of the relationship between information and the formation of attitudes.

Source: Adapted from D. Katz et al., *Food: Where Nutrition, Politics & Culture Meet* (Washington: Center for Science in the Public Interest, 1976).

PART B: Understanding Hunger as a Complex Issue: Creating a Concept Web (45 minutes)

1. Brainstorm with participants a list of terms (e.g., causes, descriptions, events) that they associate with hunger. Write these in a list on the board.

2. After generating a substantial list, involve the participants as "concepts" in creating a three dimensional web. Ask each participant to be one of the terms and attach a paper label to her/himself. **Note:** This might have to be done in several groups depending on the number of participants.

3. Discuss how these words relate to each other. Ask participants to describe the nature and direction of the relationship. Encourage participants to consider the interactive nature of these factors (e.g., hunger contributes to illness and illness to hunger). Then have them make connections among each other using pieces of yarn. Have them discuss the relationship as they extend the yarn.

4. As the group becomes a web of concepts and yarn, ask them to identify the essential relationships that must be addressed if hunger is to be eliminated in our nation and the world.

   Some concepts to consider for the hunger web: hunger, illness, gender, malnutrition, poverty, welfare, race/racism, disability, charity, success/failure in school, population, government policies, public attitudes, foreign aid, crop surplus, employment opportunities, human rights.

Source: Adapted from Sonja William, *Exploding the Hunger Myths* (San Francisco: Institute for Food and Development Policy, 1987).

PART C: What Are the Effects of...? (45 minutes)

This activity, a variant of a concept web, uses factual statements related to hunger or poverty as a point of departure and challenges participants to think through multiple consequences. **Note:** You may need to demonstrate this way of thinking by working through one statement with the whole group.

1. Divide participants into pairs or small groups and assign each one of the statements from Handout 1, *Statements about Hunger and Poverty*. Assign more than one group the same statement to promote later discussion.

2. Have participants generate as many effects as possible for the statement(s) assigned. They should organize their response to the assignment in the following manner:

   a. Write the initial statement in a circle in the center of the paper.

   b. Identify three immediate consequences that result. Write these in circles around the initial statement circle. Connect these by lines with arrows.

   c. Next, identify two secondary consequences that might result from each of these three immediate effects. Write them in circles too and connect them with arrows from the immediate consequences circles.

   d. Then, continue the process with two tertiary consequences that might grow out of each secondary one.

3. Have pairs who worked on the same statement join to compare and discuss the effects they develop from the same statement.

4. Ask a spokesperson from each group to summarize their effects, including the differences between pairs.

   • Invite the whole group to suggest other possible causal relationships.

   • Discuss the process of tracing the effects of a statement.

     a. Were there any surprising results?

     b. Were all the results serious? Possible? Likely? Why or why not?

     c. What did participants discover in doing this kind of consequential thinking? Could this method be applied to any aspects of their personal lives?

5. Debrief the activity drawing on these questions to guide discussion:

- How are children affected by the condition described in the statement?

- Does to condition described affect both males and females equally?

- What effects might this condition have on our economy?

- What are some of the short and long term effects of the condition described?

- Who has or does not have these human rights in our society?

- What do we learn from this activity about what happens when people enjoy certain human rights? When they are denied their rights?

- How does knowing that this condition exists affect you?

- If we know there are people in this community/nation/world who are hungry and undernourished but do nothing to help, can we call ourselves moral, caring human beings?

6. **Research:**

Use the Internet and library sources to find out if any of the imagined consequences are, in fact, true. (See *Organizations Working for Economic and Social Justice,* p. 106).

PART D: Family Budget Activity (45 minutes)

1. Pass out copies of Handout 2, *Family Budget Sheet* and explain that this is a monthly budget for a family of three (two parents and one child).

2. Read the following aloud from Handout 2, *Family Budget Sheet:* Imagine that this is your family. Like other families in similar situations, yours will have to make difficult decisions about how to spend your money. Every month you have to make choices about how to meet all your financial responsibilities, including feeding your children. Currently your budget contains no room for luxuries, such as entertainment or a car.

3. Go over the items on the list, stressing that the family lives from month to month with no savings to help them meet an emergency.

4. Divide participants into six small groups and assign each group a budget sheet and one of the three situations at the bottom of the sheet. Explain that the group must respond to the situation by reworking their family's budget in the second column.

5. After the groups have revised their budgets, ask groups with the same situation to join together to compare their revised budgets. Do they differ? How and why?

6. Discuss this budget-making with the whole group, using some of these questions:

   • Is this budget realistic (e.g., is this a realistic amount for rent, food, clothing, utilities, and transportation in your community)?

   • Do people in your community actually live on so little money? **Note:** if possible, obtain information about income levels in your community.

   • What do people do when they cannot meet their expenses?

   • Is any help available for people who cannot meet their expenses?

   • How would living on a budget like this affect the family's human rights? Which of those found in the UDHR? Explain.

Source: Adapted from: Dorosin, Geelan, Gordon, and Moore, *Why is There Hunger in Our Community?* (Oakland: Alameda County Community Food Bank, 1997).

PART E: Taking Action (Variable)

1. There are many ways in which participants can become directly involved in attacking the problem of hunger. A very partial list includes raising money for an organization, collecting food for a foodshelf, volunteering at the foodshelf, educating others via posters, newspaper articles, videos about conditions in your community, nation, or world, and writing to public officials (local and national) advocating for certain policies.

2. See the activity *Community Survey and Action Plan*, p. 42, for research questions to inform the development of an action plan.

3. See Appendices, p. 106, for a list of organizations working to address hunger and related problems.

Source:
Written by David Shiman.

HUNGER AND POVERTY STATEMENTS

1. The human right to an adequate diet is not legally recognized in the United States.

2. 40,000 children in the world die of causes related to hunger and poverty every day.

3. Approximately 25% of the homeless in the USA are children.

4. Over half of all families living in poverty in the United States are maintained by women only.

5. Unemployment rates for Native, African, and Latino/a Americans are considerably higher than those for most other US citizens.

6. Average weekly earnings for Native, African, and Latino/a Americans are considerably lower than those for most other US citizens.

7. The Food Stamp program serves more than 25 million people in the United States.

8. One in six elderly citizens in the USA is either hungry or has an inadequate diet.

9. One in four children comes to school undernourished in the United States.

10. More than 3/4 of the world's starving people are women and their dependent children.

11. During the past two decades at least, the gap between the rich and the poor in the United States has grown wider.

12. School Breakfast Programs serve 7 million children daily while School Lunch Programs serve over 26 million each day in the United States.

13. Prices in supermarkets are generally higher in low income than in middle income neighborhoods.

14. There is enough food in the world to feed everyone, but there are still millions who are hungry.

15. There was a potato famine in Ireland in the middle of the 19th century that caused several million Irish to emigrate to the United States.

16. During the Depression in the 1930s in the USA, there was a "dust bowl" in the midwest and most crops could not be grown for several years.

Sources: US Department of Commerce, Bureau of the Census, Statistical Abstract of the United States (yearly); World Bank, World Development Report, NY: Oxford University Press, (yearly); UNICEF, The State of the World's Children (yearly); Bread for the World (1998); *US Hunger and Poverty Report,* 1100 Wayne Avenue, Suite 1000, Silver Spring, MD, 20910; *The New Internationalist,* No 310 (March 1999).

ACTIVITY 5: HANDOUT 2

FAMILY BUDGET SHEET

Imagine that this is your family. Like other families in similar situations, yours will have to make difficult decisions about how to spend your money. Every month you have to make choices about how to meet all your financial responsibilities, including feeding your children. Currently your budget contains no room for luxuries, such as entertainment or a car.

Item	Column #1	Column #2
Rent (2 bedroom apartment)	$800.00	
Phone	$40.00	
Gas, Water & Garbage	$60.00	
Groceries	$380.00	
Transportation (2 Bus Passes)	$60.00	
Entertainment		
Medical Care (addition to basic employer coverage)	$60.00	
Savings		
Other		
Total Expenditures	$1,400.00	
Monthly Income	$1,400.00	
Balance	$0.00	

Situation 1: Your child gets sick. The doctor's visit, the tests, and the medication costs are $300.00 more than what your employer paid health insurance will cover. How will you pay the medical bills?

Situation 2: You lose your job. The unemployment benefits, which begin one week after your last pay check arrives is only equal to two-thirds of your regular pay. Your total monthly income decreases by $400.00. How will you balance your budget?

Situation 3: You catch the flu and miss four days of work. Without paid sick leave, your income is reduced by $160.00. How will you make up for this shortfall in your budget?

Source: Dorosin, Geelan, Gordon, and Moore, *Why is There Hunger in Our Community?* (Oakland: Alameda County Community Food Bank, 1997). Used with permission.

ACTIVITY 6

THE ELDERLY POOR

OVERVIEW

This activity focuses on some of the human rights concerns of those who are old and poor in the USA. It draws on data from US Census and case studies to highlight the issues and provides opportunities for local interviewing and the development of participant action projects.

Time:	1-3 hours
Materials:	• Copies of Universal Declaration of Human Rights (UDHR)
	• Handout 1, *Facts about the Elderly Population in the United States*
	• Handout 2, *Three Case Studies*
	• Handout 3, *Questions on Human Dignity*
	• Blackboard or chart paper, chalk or markers
Setting:	High school – Adult groups

PROCEDURE

1. Distribute the abbreviated list of the Universal Declaration of Human Rights.
   Note: This activity assumes some understanding of human rights and the UDHR. If this is not the case, provide basic background information, such as the brief history included in this book, concentrating on the theme of "those rights/needs to which everyone is entitled."

2. Ask participants to identify needs that seem to become increasingly important to people as they grow old in this country. Briefly discuss their reasons for selection. Ask how these needs would be affected if the aging person were also poor.

3. Ask participants which of these needs they think are also human rights. Encourage participants to refer to the articles in the UDHR. Make a chart of those needs identified as human rights and label it "HUMAN RIGHTS/NEEDS."

4. Move deeper into the topic through the following questions:

   • In what ways might income level, sex, race or ethnicity, disability, age, location of residence (urban/rural) affect the sorts of concerns that an elderly person might have? **Note:** Divide into groups for a brief discussion with each assigned one characteristic.

- Would the list of concerns generated above be any different from the list one might develop for people in their thirties or forties? Explain.

- What kinds of services (e.g., medical, housing, transportation) do people tend to need more often as they grow older?

- What special kinds of living conditions (e.g., buildings with elevators, wheelchair access, social support) are older people more likely to need?

- Which of the human rights identified above are in danger of being violated, of being denied, and in need of protection?

5. Distribute Handout 1, *Facts about the Elderly Population in the United States*. Ask participants to decide whether or not these facts match with their earlier statements. Ask them to identify additional facts that they need to determine the accuracy of their statements. Ask participants to generate non-statistical factors that affect one's wellbeing, such as feeling valued or discounted, happy or sad, lonely or included, competent or helpless, and loved or rejected, that might also shed light on the conditions of the elderly.

6. Divide class into groups and assign each a case study from Handout 2, *Three Case Studies*. Ask them to complete Handout 3, *Questions on Human Dignity*. Explain that they have thirty minutes to complete this task. Check with each group to be sure they understand the instructions and have established a note-taking procedure. Remind them when ten minutes and five minutes remain.

7. Read each question and ask for a representative from one group to summarize their discussion. Ask other groups to report only where their conclusions differed. If time is limited, focus on the final three questions.

   a. What issues do these case studies raise for you about human dignity? About the relationship between human rights and human needs? Between rights and responsibilities?

   b. Do these factors affect the making of local and national policies aimed at helping the elderly achieve full human rights? Encourage the participants to consider other factors as well.

   - compassion
   - consensus
   - social class attitudes
   - economic/financial considerations
   - silence/invisibility
   - media treatment
   - sense of justice
   - indifference
   - use or absence of power
   - morality
   - political considerations

8. Prepare the groups to interview elderly persons in their community. This involves identifying interviewees and creating a list of questions. These interviews might be a building block for the development of a participant action plan to address the human rights needs of the elderly poor in their community. (See Step 10, Taking Action below.)

9. Encourage participants to summarize their learnings about the inter-related nature of human needs and rights and the challenges confronting the elderly poor in this society. They might wish to learn more about some of the following topics:

   • Opportunities for the elderly to supplement social security or pension income;

   • Community outreach and educational programs for the elderly;

   • Social Security and Medicare: past, present, and future challenges;

   • Gender and aging: attitudes, demographics, and income characteristics;

   • Residence patterns in the community: living alone, with family, or in nursing homes; and

   • An historical perspective on growing old in the community.

10. Taking Action

   Have participants consider the questions below as building blocks for developing an action plan on behalf of the elderly poor. **Note:** Refer to the activity *Community Research and Action Plan,* p. 42, for additional questions and a framework for developing an action project.

   • Would Raffi Hagopian, Laura Templeton, and Jose Flores (the cases in Handout 2, *Three Case Studies*) find support for their needs in your community?

   • Are there people with similar concerns living in your community? What support do they get and from whom?

   • Are there elderly clients of social services agencies who can help them assess the services from a human rights perspective?

   • Is there anything that the participant group can do to promote and defend the human rights of the elderly poor in their community?

Source: Written by Sushanna Ellington, Human Rights Educators Network, Amnesty International USA, and David Shiman. Adapted from F. Pratt, *Education for Aging: A Teacher's Source Book* (Acton, MA: McCarthy-Towne School, 1981).

FACTS ABOUT THE ELDERLY POPULATION IN THE UNITED STATES

Note: The term elderly refers to people 65 years of age and older.

LIVING AND DYING

- **Growing Numbers**: In 1997, there were 31.9 million elderly people: 13.4 million men and 18.5 million women. That's eleven times more people over 65 years than in 1900. The number under 65 years has only tripled since then.

- **Living Longer**: In 1776, life expectancy was 35 years. By 1996, life expectancy had climbed to 76 years. Women average 79 years, with whites living until 80 and African Americans to 74 years. Men average 73 years, with whites living until 74 and African Americans to 66 years.

- **Reaching 65:** Those reaching 65 years can expect, on the average, to live another 17 years. Again, this varies by sex and race. White women have 19 more years, but African American Women have 17 more. White men have 15.7 more years but African American men 13.6 more.

- **More Women:** For every 100 women who are 65 years or older, there are 69 men. Among those 85 years or older, there are only 39 men for every 100 women.

- **Alone or Together:** 75% of elderly men living outside institutions (like nursing homes) have a spouse; 41% of elderly women do. When health fails, elderly men are likely to have a spouse for support; elderly women more often live and die alone. And, the older one gets, the greater the need for help bathing, getting around the house, and preparing meals. In 1993, eight of ten elderly people living alone (outside institutions) were women.

STAYING HEALTHY AND SAFE

- **Health Care Needs:** Approximately 80% of the elderly population will face at least one of the following chronic, limiting illnesses or conditions: heart disorders, arthritis, diabetes, osteoporosis, senile dementia, and ones that affect respiratory and digestive systems.

- **Doctors and Hospitals:** On average, persons between 65-74 years visit doctors five times per year and those over 75 years visit six times. (**Note:** Those between 22-44 years averaged two visits per annum.) In addition, the majority of those 65 years and over had hospital care in the past five years (1994).

- **Insurance:** Virtually all (99%) those over 65 years have health insurance, 96% having Medicare. This percentage is higher than for those under 65 years. However, insurance coverage is increasingly inadequate for many elderly person's needs; poor elderly people report having to choose between buying food or buying medicine.

- **Nutrition Programs:** In 1995, over 250 million meals were provided elderly people through federally supported programs. Nearly one half of these went to those who were homebound due to disability, illness, or geographic isolation. Still, many poor elderly people report skipping meals because of a lack of food and money.

- **Food Stamp Programs:** In 1995, coupons were used by 2 million elderly people, but only 35% of eligible elderly persons had applied for them.

- **Physical Safety:** Elderly persons feel particularly vulnerable to crime, with 55% afraid to walk alone at night. Only 40% of 40-49 year olds had similar fears.

PAYING THE BILLS

- **Poverty:** Approximately one out of every ten elderly persons was living in official poverty in 1996. This is between three and four million people. About 14% of elderly women and 7% of elderly men were officially poor. Also, 9.4% of the elderly whites, 25.3% of elderly African Americans, 24.4% for Hispanics were poor. And, for all groups, the older you get, the more likely it is you will become poor.

- **Median Income:** The median income for elderly men in 1996 was $16,886 for whites, $11,570 for African Americans, and $9,794 for Hispanics. The median incomes of elderly women were substantially less: $9,654 for whites, $7,067 for African Americans, and $6,652 for Hispanics.

- **Social Security:** For many, social security is all they have. However, some, have other means of support: interest (67%), pensions (32%), dividends (20%), wages & salaries (14%), and rents, royalties, and trusts (11%).

- **Housing:** The overwhelming majority of elderly people live in households not in institutions. Half of the elderly poor spend 50% or more of their income in housing costs. Over 1/3 of all federally subsidized housing is occupied by older persons.

Sources: U.S. Department of Commerce, Bureau of the Census, Statistical Abstract of the United States (yearly); U.S. Dept. of Commerce, Bureau of the Census, *Sixty-Five Plus in the United States,* 1995; Yntema,S. (Ed.) *Americans 55 & Older: A Changing Market,* Ithaca, NY: New Strategist Publications, 1997; Weimer, J.P *Many Elderly at Nutritional Risk, Food Review* 20:1 (Jan.-April 1997), 42-48.

THREE CASE STUDIES

Case Study #1: Mr Raffi Hagopian

Baltimore, Maryland: The winter sun strained to enter through the grimy window of the eleventh floor studio apartment where Raffi Hagopian, seventy-nine, was beginning to awaken underneath the broken acrylic electric blanket which barely insulates him from the fifty-five degree temperature in the room.

For Mr. Hagopian and millions of other elderly poor who survive on meager social security checks, this is the most risky time of the month--the week before the next check arrives and when this month's money is completely gone.

Until the next check arrives in five days, Mr. Hagopian has no clean underwear or shirt or pants to change into. His towels and sheets are also soiled, rendering them unusable for the moment. His coins for the laundry were used up a week ago.

His only food is packets of fast food condiments—mayonnaise and mustard and cellophane wrapped hot sauce. His only appliance is a used one-burner hot plate. There is no stove or refrigerator in the room. Down the hall, the sink and toilet and single shower are shared, in turn, by his neighbors who are mostly young couples with small children. Dressing quickly, he knows that the cold air in the room will further irritate his sore throat and watering eyes. He is embarrassed by his need to go to the neighborhood dining room where he will receive yet another donated meal and have to ask the volunteers for permission to use the bathroom's hot water, hand soap, and paper towels in order to clean himself.

An introvert by nature, Mr. Hagopian is a prisoner of his own shyness, who has survived adversity with a tenacious independence. His only socializing is intermittent and casual with the teenage volunteers and members of their parents' generation at the neighborhood church dining hall. Yet, there has never been an occasion when he has felt comfortable asking these well-intentioned volunteers to help him problem-solve his basic need for services and information. And his only occasional appearance at the dining hall makes the church's outreach more difficult to achieve.

Ironically, Mr. Hagopian worked his entire adult life, supporting a wife and son (both of whom died in the 1970s) until a work-related disability forced his retirement at age sixty-seven. He rarely received health benefits from his employers, and since his retirement he is unfamiliar with how to access medical services, including physical therapy needed for his disability. He has not had his eyes examined, his teeth cleaned, or a physical examination for more than fifteen years. He is reluctant to use the city bus system for fear of becoming lost or disoriented if he leaves these familiar surroundings. He fears for his safety whenever he goes out at night.

Like many of his generation, Mr. Hagopian's isolation is a result of several factors, including a rugged individualism honed by years of blue collar work ethic and an aversion to asking for public assistance of any kind. Yet, his current living situation is unmanageable without some intervention that will provide medical, nutritional, and other essential services to which he is entitled but is not currently receiving.

Case Study #2: Mrs. Laura Templeton

Vallejo, California: In the "gray ghetto" of the largely deserted town center, the seventy-three year old former employee of the C & H Sugar refinery worries that her meager pension will not keep up with the rent increase she expects for her hotel room. Mrs. Templeton is a recently widowed retiree whose savings were depleted along with her home equity in order to keep her husband, who suffered from Alzheimer's disease, at home in her care until his death.

Hoping to find at least part-time work to supplement her income, she moved from the company town of Crockett, CA, to nearby Vallejo in the late 1980s. However, the city's economic prosperity was critically depressed with the closure of its principal employer—Mare Island Naval Shipyard—a San Francisco Bay Area naval installation which had employed thousands of skilled workers on a 24-hour schedule. Its closure closely coincided with her relocation and eliminated her prospects of finding work as a housekeeper or child care provider for one of the many two-income Mare Island families with small children. Now, she is stuck in a downtown area that has lost many of its small businesses to which Mrs. Templeton could walk from her apartment.

She faces a whole new set of challenges: the unpredictability of this place and a lack of knowledge of how to access the services that might guide her through this time of transition toward independence. In fact, the city has moved its offices away from the center of the downtown in order to meet the needs of families in neighborhoods to the east of the interstate highway that divides old town from new developments. There is public transportation; however, Mrs. Templeton is confused by the system and afraid of becoming lost in one of the more volatile neighborhoods to the north of the town center.

She often skips meals rather than going out alone at night. The prices and quality of food in the neighborhood convenience markets limit her ability to shop for a balanced diet and to budget her money for other purposes. Mrs. Templeton is isolated and invisible to those who might have services to address at least some of her needs.

Case Study #3: Mr. Jose Flores

Chimayo, New Mexico: As a young child in the 1920s, Mr. Flores emigrated from the Philippines along with his father, uncle, and two older brothers. Although he has a working knowledge of English, Mr. Flores never received formal schooling in either Tagalog or

English; therefore, he is reluctant to sign anything he cannot read or to reveal to strangers the extent to which he is illiterate.

Instead of attending school, Mr. Flores worked in the agriculture fields of the American Southwest, moving constantly from rural farm to orchard across six states in a seasonal cycle that made one year blend seamlessly with the next. Over the years, he has picked everything from tomatoes and strawberries to pecans and cotton.

Due to the Asian exclusion acts and other discriminatory practices in the 19th and 20th centuries that forbade Filipino workers from marrying outside of their own culture and the immigration policies which made it nearly impossible to unite separated families or to allow for unmarried females to enter the country, Mr. Flores never married. In fact, he lost contact with many relatives due to his lack of formal education and the missed opportunities for written communication.

The years of abusive working conditions—the lack of sanitation and nutritious food, the rigors of stoop labor, and the exposure to pesticides in the field—have taken their toll on Mr. Flores' overall health and sense of well-being.

He is reclusive, living alone on land that is physically near an urban center, but the layout of Santa Fe is just too confusing for him to access. His small savings will not keep him warm and fed for more than another year.

QUESTIONS ABOUT HUMAN DIGNITY

1. Choose someone to read the case study aloud to your group. As you listen, look for evidence in the case that an elderly person's human right to affordable housing, adequate nutrition, and/or health case is at risk or has been denied. Refer to the lists of human rights/needs generated earlier.

2. Discuss the following questions and take notes on your answers, if possible, with a different note taker for each question.

   • Is human dignity compromised in your case study?

   • Are any of the human rights listed earlier being denied? Refer to the articles of the UDHR.

   • Where would you find the roots of these specific human rights abuses? The individual person and his/her family? Government? Former employers? Societal values? Nature of the economic system?

   • Is there evidence that any human rights listed earlier are being protected in these cases? If so, name the rights which are protected. Who or what protects them?

   • Are the problems identified ones that can be addressed by the efforts of a social service agency or charitable organization? Why or why not?

   • Where does responsibility lie for the care and protection of the human rights of vulnerable, elderly people?

   • How might these cases be different if US government policy considered the social and economic rights to adequate housing, nutrition, and health care, found in Article 25 of UDHR, to be human rights to which everyone is entitled?

   • What issues does this case study raise for you about human dignity? About the relationship between human rights and human needs? Between rights and responsibilities?

ACTIVITY 7

TAKING THE HUMAN RIGHTS
TEMPERATURE OF YOUR SCHOOL

Participants evaluate their school's human rights climate using criteria derived from the Universal Declaration of Human Rights. The subsequent discussion builds towards identifying areas of particular concern and developing an action plan to begin addressing them. This activity can be easily adapted for assessing the human rights temperature of one's family, neighborhood, or other community group.

Time:	1-2 hours
Materials:	• Handout 1, *Taking the Human Rights Temperature* • UDHR (reference only)
Setting:	Middle and high school – Administrators, parents, and teachers

PROCEDURE

1. Have participants evaluate their school's human rights climate, (e.g., take its "temperature") by completing the survey questionnaire below. Prior to completing the instrument or developing an action plan, participants might conduct research into school conditions, using the survey items below.

2. Prepare for discussion by creating a 1-4 rating scale on a chalkboard or newsprint. Then have participants call out responses to each item. **Important:** Participants might not wish to make their own responses public. Consider collecting the questionnaires and redistributing them so that participant anonymity can be assured.

3. Discuss the findings from the survey, drawing on the following questions to move from analysis and evaluation to the development of an action plan.

   a. In which areas does your school appear to be adhering to or promoting human rights principles?

   b. In which areas do there seem to be human rights problems? Which of these are of particular concern to you? Elaborate on the areas of concern, providing examples and identifying patterns in human rights violations.

c. How do you explain the existence of such problematic conditions?

- Do they have race/ethnicity, class, gender, disability, age, or sexual orientation dimensions?

- Are the issues related to participation in decision-making (who is included and who isn't)?

- Who benefits and who loses/suffers as a result of the existing human rights violations?

- Other explanations to consider?

d. Have you or any other members of your community contributed in any way to the construction and perpetuation of the existing climate (e.g., by acting or not acting in certain ways, by ignoring abuses or not reporting incidents)?

e. Were those completing the questionnaire representative of the population of the school? Would you expect different results from a different group of people? In what ways might another group's responses differ and why? Should these differences be of any concern to you and to the school community? When determining which human rights concerns need to be addressed and how to address them, how can you be certain to take into account the perspectives and experiences of different people?

f. What needs to be done to improve the human rights climate in your school? What action(s) can you and your group take to create a more humane and just environment where human rights values are promoted and human rights behaviors practiced?

4. Review questionnaire item #25, stressing the importance of assuming responsibility and acting. Then, as a group brainstorm possible actions the group might take to improve the human rights situation? Decide on a short list of options for action. Thoroughly debate and discuss the short list before deciding on actions to be taken.

5. Based on the group discussion, choose items for action and develop an action plan, identifying goals, strategies and responsibilities.

TAKING THE HUMAN RIGHTS TEMPERATURE OF YOUR SCHOOL

Introduction

The questions below are adapted from the United Nations Universal Declaration of Human Rights (UDHR). The relevant UDHR Articles are included parenthetically in each statement. Some of these issues correlate more directly to the UDHR than others. All of these questions are related to the fundamental human right to education found in Article 26 of the Universal Declaration. It asserts:

> *Everyone has the right to education... Education shall be directed to the full development of the human personality and to the strengthening of respect for human rights and fundamental freedoms.*

When discrimination is mentioned in the questionnaire below, it refers to a wide range of conditions: race, ethnicity/culture, sex, physical/intellectual capacities, friendship associations, age, culture, disability, social class/financial status, physical appearance, sexual orientation, life style choices, nationality, and living space. Although this is a much more expansive list than that found in the Universal Declaration of Human Rights, it is more helpful in assessing the human rights temperature in your school community.

The results should provide a general sense of the school's climate in light of principles found in the Universal Declaration of Human Rights. Obviously more questions are needed and follow-up questioning during the discussion will enrich the assessment. These questions can help to identify specific areas of concern that need to be addressed.

Source: Adapted from David Shiman, *Teaching Human Rights* (Denver: Center for Teaching International Relations, University of Denver, 1999). Written with Kristi Rudelius-Palmer.

THE QUESTIONS

Directions

Take the human rights temperature of your school. Read each statement and assess how accurately it describes your school community in the blank next to it. (Keep in mind all members of your school: participants, teachers, administrators, staff.) At the end, total up your score to determine your overall assessment score for your school.

1	2	3	4	DN
no/never	rarely	often	yes/always	don't know

_____ 1. My school is a place where participants are safe and secure. (Art. 3 & 5)

_____ 2. All participants receive equal information and encouragement about academic and career opportunities. (Art. 2)

_____ 3. Members of the school community are not discriminated against because of their life style choices, such as manner of dress, association with certain people, and non-school activities. (Arts. 2 & 16)

_____ 4. My school provides equal access, resources, activities, and scheduling accommodations for all individuals. (Arts. 2 & 7)

_____ 5. Members of my school community will oppose discriminatory or demeaning actions, materials, or slurs in the school. (Arts. 2, 3, 7, 28, & 29)

_____ 6. When someone demeans or violates the rights of another person, the violator is helped to learn how to change his/her behavior. (Art. 26)

_____ 7. Members of my school community care about my full human as well as academic development and try to help me when I am in need. (Arts. 3, 22, 26 & 29)

_____ 8. When conflicts arise, we try to resolve them through non-violent ways. (Arts. 3, 28)

_____ 9. Institutional policies and procedures are implemented when complaints of harassment or discrimination are submitted. (Arts. 3 & 7)

_____ 10. In matters related to discipline (including suspension and expulsion), all persons are assured of fair, impartial treatment in the determination of guilt and assignment of punishment. (Arts. 6, 7, 8, 9 & 10)

_____ 11. No one in our school is subjected to degrading treatment or punishment. (Art. 5)

_____ 12. Someone accused of wrong doing is presumed innocent until proven guilty. (Art. 11)

_____ 13. My personal space and possessions are respected. (Arts. 12 & 17)

_____ 14. My school community welcomes participants, teachers, administrators, and staff from diverse backgrounds and cultures, including people not born in the USA. (Arts. 2, 6,13, 14 & 15)

_____ 15. I have the liberty to express my beliefs and ideas (political, religious, cultural, or other) without fear of discrimination. (Art. 19)

_____ 16. Members of my school can produce and disseminate publications without fear of censorship or punishment. (Art. 19)

_____ 17. Diverse voices and perspectives (e.g., gender, race/ethnicity, ideological) are represented in courses, textbooks, assemblies, libraries, and classroom instruction. (Arts. 2, 19, & 27)

_____ 18. I have the opportunity to express my culture through music, art, and literary form. (Art. 19, 27 & 28)

_____ 19. Members of my school have the opportunity to participate (individually and through associations) in democratic decision making processes to develop school policies and rules. (Arts. 20, 21, & 23)

_____ 20. Members of my school have the right to form associations within the school to advocate for their rights or the rights of others. (Arts. 19, 20, & 23)

_____ 21. Members of my school encourage each other to learn about societal and global problems related to justice, ecology, poverty, and peace. (Preamble & Arts. 26 & 29)

_____ 22. Members of my school encourage each other to organize and take action to address societal and global problems related to justice, ecology, poverty, and peace. (Preamble & Arts. 20 & 29)

_____ 23. Members of my school community are able to take adequate rest/recess time during the school day and work reasonable hours under fair work conditions. (Arts. 23 & 24)

_____ 24. Employees in my school are paid enough to have a standard of living adequate for the health and well-being (including housing, food, necessary social services and security from unemployment, sickness and old age) of themselves and their families. (Arts. 22 & 25)

_____ 25. I take responsibility in my school to ensure other individuals do not discriminate and that they behave in ways that promote the safety and well being of my school community. (Arts. 1 & 29)

TEMPERATURE POSSIBLE   =   100 HUMAN RIGHTS DEGREES

YOUR SCHOOL'S TEMPERATURE_____

MARTIN LUTHER KING JR. – FROM CIVIL RIGHTS TO HUMAN RIGHTS

Through this activity, participants examine Dr. King's essay entitled "The World House" to learn how his vision and commitment to action transcend US-specific civil rights issues to include human rights that affect all people.

Time:	2-3 hours
Materials:	• Blackboard or chart paper, chalk or markers
	• Handout 1, *The World House*
	• Copies of the Universal Declaration of Human Rights (UDHR)
	• Optional: copies of the national Constitution
Setting:	Middle school – Adult groups

PROCEDURE

PART A: Who was Martin Luther King, Jr.? (1 hour)

1. **Brainstorm:**

   Ask the group what they know or remember about Martin Luther King. Record their responses on the blackboard or chart paper as two lists under the headings "BIOGRAPHY" and "HUMAN RIGHTS ISSUES." Be sure to leave ample room on the "Issues" chart to add text to the right of each item. Retain the charts for further use. Your charts might look like this.

BIOGRAPHY	HUMAN RIGHTS ISSUES
Was assassinated	Racial equality
Advocated non-violence	Right to vote
Worked among Blacks in the USA	Right to equal use of public services
Won Nobel Peace Prize	Right to non-violent assembly
Was a Christian minister	Right to a living wage

Note: If participants lack information about King, you might ask them to interview elders in preparation for discussion and/or add a few important biographical facts. However, do not add to the list of issues.

2. **Analyze:**

Read aloud the list of issues the group has generated. Explain that rights are generally categorized in two groups, civil/political and social/economic rights. Explain these definitions and/or write them on the chart. Ask the group to determine which category each of the issues listed belongs to and mark each issue "C/P" or "S/E." This list will be predominantly civil/political rights.

CIVIL AND POLITICAL RIGHTS: The rights of citizens to liberty and equality, sometimes referred to as first generation rights. Civil rights include freedom to worship, to think and express oneself, to vote, to take part in political life, and to have access to information.

SOCIAL AND ECONOMIC RIGHTS: Rights that give people social and economic security, sometimes referred to as security-oriented or second-generation rights. Examples are the right to food, shelter, and health care. There is disagreement whether the government is obligated to provide these benefits.

3. **Compare:**

Introduce and distribute the Universal Declaration of Human Rights (UDHR), explaining that it is the United Nations' fundamental document that defines human rights for all the peoples of the world. Ask participants to find articles in the UDHR that match each issue listed. Encourage participants to read aloud the article they find. Enter each on the chart.

Optional: You may wish to repeat this step using the Constitution and its Amendments. Note significant differences, if any, between the two documents.

SAMPLE CHART

ISSUES	UDHR Articles	CONSTITUTION Articles/Amendments
Racial equality (C/P)	Art. #_____	_____
Right to vote (C/P)	Art. #_____	_____
Right to equal use of public services (C/P)	Art. #_____	_____
Right to non-violent assembly (C/P)	Art. #_____	_____
Right to living wage (S/E)	Art. #_____	_____

PART B: From Civil Rights to Human Rights (1 hour or more)

1. **Set the Context:**

   Explain that although most people associate Martin Luther King with civil rights in the United States, he actually had a broader vision that included all human rights and all human beings (even though the language he used was not always gender inclusive).

2. **Read:**

   Divide participants into small groups. Give each group copies of "The World House" and ask them to read it aloud together. When finished, each group should make a list of any new information they have gained about Dr. King's life or the issues he worked for.

3. **Report:**

   When all groups have completed their reading, ask someone from each group to present their list and add new entries to the original lists of biographical facts and issues generated in Part A, Step 1.

4. **Analyze:**

   As in Part A, determine which of the new issues are civil/political rights or social/economic and label them. The new issues will include many more social/economic rights than the original list.

5. **Compare:**

   Repeat Part A, Step 3, matching the issues with the relevant article(s) of the UDHR and entering the article number on the chart. **Optional:** Do the same with the Constitution. Note significant differences, if any, between the two documents.

6. **Discuss:**

   Use some of the following excerpts and questions to broaden participants' understanding of the issues for which Dr. King worked. No doubt, there will be conflicting opinions on these controversial topics.

   - *Equality with whites will not solve the problems of either whites or Negroes if it means equality in a world society stricken by poverty and a universe doomed to extinction by war.*

     Why do you think Dr. King believes that racial equality is not enough for the realization of human rights?

- *All over the world like a fever, the great masses of people are determined to end the exploitation of their races and lands. They are awake and moving toward their goal like a tidal wave.*

  Dr. King wrote these words in the 1960s. Is this "tidal wave" still going on? Ask for examples that support or contradict this statement. How does this statement relate to human rights?

- *[T]he era of colonialism, is at an end.... The earth is being redistributed.*

  Do you think that power held by the so-called "western world" or former colonial powers is indeed being redistributed more fairly throughout the world? Cite examples to support your view.

- *Among the moral imperatives of our time, we are challenged to work all over the world with unshakable determination to wipe out the last vestiges of racism.*

  Why is eliminating racism a "moral imperative"? What progress has been made in eliminating racism in the world? In your country? In your community? What evidence is there that racism still exists?

- *The time has come for an all-out war against poverty. The rich nations must use their vast resources of wealth to develop the underdeveloped, school the unschooled and feed the unfed.... If they would allocate just two percent of their gross national product annually for a period of ten or twenty years for the development of the underdeveloped nations, mankind would go a long way toward conquering the ancient enemy, poverty.*

  Do rich nations indeed have a responsibility to use their wealth to help under-developed nations? What do you think of King's suggestion for a "Marshall Plan" for Asia, Africa, and South America? Does your country already contribute to the development of poorer nations? If so, what percentage of its gross national product does it contribute and how does that compare with that given by other countries? Do people have a human right to freedom from poverty? If so, whose responsibility is it to defend that right? Do rich individuals have a similar responsibility?

- *The well-off and the secure have too often become the indifferent and oblivious to the poverty and deprivation in their midst. The poor in our countries have been shut out of our minds, and driven from the mainstream of our societies, because we have allowed them to become invisible.*

  In what ways are the poor in your community treated as "invisible"? When and where are poor people likely to be found? When and where would you have personal conversation and interaction with people who are poor? Do you believe that "The well-off and the secure have too often become the indifferent and oblivious to the poverty and deprivation ..." in your community? In your country? What responsibility, if any, do "the well-off and secure" have to those who are neither?

- *A final problem that mankind must solve in order to survive in the world house that we have inherited is finding an alternative to war and human destruction.*

  Is peace a human right? Dr. King suggests that the philosophy and strategy of nonviolence is the way to end war. What do you understand by "the philosophy and strategy of nonviolence"? Do you think it can end conflict on the international level? The national or community level? The interpersonal level?

- Summarize the reasons that King gives for why rich nations should work to end poverty in poor nations. Do you agree with these reasons? Are they true for individuals as well as nations? How do King's reasons relate to human rights.

GOING FURTHER

1. **Writing**. Choose a sentence or passage from the reading and write a reflection, defending or opposing King's position. For example:

- "Oppressed people cannot remain oppressed forever."

- "In the final analysis the rich must not ignore the poor because both rich and poor are tied together. They entered the same mysterious gateway of human birth, into the same adventure of mortal life."

- "In a real sense, all life In interrelated. The agony of the poor impoverishes the rich; the betterment of the poor enriches the rich. We are inevitably our brother's keepers because we are our brother's brother. Whatever affects one directly affects all indirectly."

- "We still have a choice today; nonviolent coexistence or violent coannihilation. This may well be mankind's last chance to choose between chaos and community."

2. **Research**. These projects might be undertaken by individuals or small groups and their results shared with the whole group.

- Find out more about King's views on nonviolence.

- What people and philosophies inspired King's ideas? Did his methods work? Why or why not?

- Many criticized King's nonviolence policy. Why?

- Have nonviolent methods been used in other political crises since King?

- How is poverty defined? What proportion of the population in your country or community is "poor"?

- What kinds of people are poor? Are they predominantly of a certain race, ethnic group, age, etc.?

- What are some outcomes related to poverty (e.g., crime, disease, infant mortality, educational level, life expectancy)? How are these aspects of poverty reflected in your community?

- Compare the statistics about poverty in your community, city, region, or country to those of other communities, cities, regions, or countries. Do you live in a "poor place?"

- Find out what policies and programs your country has now to help end poverty in other countries. Are these actions effective?

- Find out what policies and programs your country or regional government is doing to help end poverty at home. Are these actions effective?

- Find out what the World Bank and the International Monitory Fund (IMF) are doing to end poverty worldwide. Are these actions effective?

2. **Taking Action**.

- Create a MLK Report Card for your community. (See Activity 7, p. 67, for ideas). Select rights concerns that emerge from group discussion, identify data to gather in your community, gather them, construct the Report Card, and distribute it in your community (local media!). Identify actions that need to be taken. Organize an action project. Use King's birthday to launch or culminate the activity.

- Find out what organizations are working in your community on the issues of racism, poverty, and nonviolence that Dr. King advocated. Choose one or two whose work you admire, contact them and find out how you can support their work.

- See other activities in this manual for ways to become involved in your community.

Source: Written by Nancy Flowers, Human Rights Educators Network, Amnesty International USA.

"The World House"

by Dr. Martin Luther King, Jr.

Some years ago a famous novelist died. Among his papers was found a list of suggested plots for future stories, the most prominently underscored being this one: "A widely separated family inherits a house in which they have to live together." This is the great new problem of mankind. We have inherited a large house, a great "world house" in which we have to live together—black and white, Easterner and Westerner, Gentile and Jew, Catholic and Protestant, Moslem and Hindu - a family unduly separated in ideas, culture and interest, who, because we can never again live apart, must learn somehow to live with each other in peace.

However deeply American Negroes are caught in the struggle to be at last at home in our homeland of the United Sates, we cannot ignore the larger world house in which we are also dwellers. Equality with whites will not solve the problems of either whites or Negroes if it means equality in a world society stricken by poverty and a universe doomed to extinction by war.

All inhabitants of the globe are now neighbors. This world-wide neighborhood has been brought into being largely as a result of the modern scientific and technological revolutions.

Along with [these technological] revolutions, we have also witnessed a world-wide freedom revolution over the last few decades.... In one sense the civil rights movement in the United States is a special American phenomenon which must be understood in the light of the American history and dealt with in terms of the American situation. But on another and more important level, what is happening in the United States today is a significant part of a world development.

All over the world like a fever, the great masses of people are determined to end the exploitation of their races and lands. They are awake and moving toward their goal like a tidal wave. You can hear them rumbling in every village street, on the docks, in the houses, among the participants, in the churches, and at political meetings. For several centuries the direction of history flowed from the nations and the societies of western Europe out into the rest of the world in "conquests" of various sorts. That period, the era of colonialism, is at an end. East is moving West. The earth is being redistributed. Yes, we are "shifting our basic outlooks."

These developments should not surprise any participant of history. Oppressed people cannot remain oppressed forever. The yearning for freedom eventually manifests itself....

One of the great liabilities of history is that all too many people fail to remain awake through great periods of social change. Every society has its protectors of the status quo and its fraternities of the indifferent who are notorious for sleeping through revolutions. But today our very survival depends on our ability to stay awake, to adjust to new ideas, to remain vigilant and to face the challenge of change. The large house in which we live demands that we transform this world-wide neighborhood into a world-wide brotherhood. Together we must learn to live as brother or together we will be forced to perish as fools....

II.

Among the moral imperatives of our time, we are challenged to work all over the world with unshakable determination to wipe out the last vestiges of racism ... that hound of hell which dogs the tracks of our civilization....

Another grave problem that must be solved if we are to live creatively in our world house is that of poverty on an international scale. Like a monstrous octopus, it stretches its choking, prehensile tentacles into lands and villages all over the world. Two-thirds of the peoples of the world go to bed hungry at night. They are undernourished, ill-housed and shabbily clad. Many of them have no houses or beds to sleep in. Their only beds are the sidewalks of the cities and the dusty roads of the villages. Most of these poverty-stricken children of God have never seen a physician or a dentist.

There is nothing new about poverty. What is new, however, is that we now have the resources to get rid of it.... Why should there be hunger and privation in any land, in any city, at any table, when man has the resources and the scientific know-how to provide all mankind with the basic necessities of life? ... There is no deficit in human resources; the deficit is in human will....

The time has come for an all-out war against poverty. The rich nations must use their vast resources of wealth to develop the underdeveloped, school the unschooled and feed the unfed. The well-off and the secure have too often become the indifferent and oblivious to the poverty and deprivation in their midst. The poor in our countries have been shut out of our minds, and driven from the mainstream of our societies, because we have allowed them to become invisible. Ultimately a great nation is a compassionate nation. No individual or nation can be great if it does not have a concern of "the least of these."

The first step in the world-wide war against poverty is passionate commitment.... The wealthy nations of the world must promptly initiate a massive, sustained Marshall Plan for Asia, Africa and South America. If they would allocate just two percent of their gross national product annually for a period of ten or twenty years for the development of the underdeveloped nations, mankind would go a long way toward conquering the ancient enemy, poverty....

... In the final analysis the rich must not ignore the poor because both rich and poor are tied together. They entered the same mysterious gateway of human birth, into the same adventure of mortal life.

All men are interdependent. Every nation is an heir of a vast treasure of ideas and labor to which both the living and the dead of all nations have contributed.... We are everlasting debtors to known and unknown men and women....

In a real sense, all life in interrelated. The agony of the poor impoverishes the rich; the bet-

In a real sense, all life in interrelated. The agony of the poor impoverishes the rich; the betterment of the poor enriches the rich. We are inevitably our brother's keepers because we are our brother's brother. Whatever affects one directly affects all indirectly.

A final problem that mankind must solve in order to survive in the world house that we have inherited is finding an alternative to war and human destruction.... Therefore I suggest that the philosophy and strategy of nonviolence become immediately a subject for study and for serious experimentation in every field of human conflict, by no means excluding the relations between nations.... We still have a choice today; nonviolent coexistence or violent coannihilation This may well be mankind's last chance to choose between chaos and community.

Source: King Jr,, M.L., *Where Do We Go from Here: Chaos or Community?* (New York: Harper & Row, Publishers, 1967).

> *We are all bound up together in one great bundle of humanity, and society cannot trample on the weakest and feeblest of its members without receiving the curse in its own soul.*
>
> Frances Ellen Watkins Harper

ACTIVITY 9

<u>ACTIVISTS FOR HUMAN RIGHTS</u>

OVERVIEW

This activity involves learning about the struggle for human rights through the study of biographies of rights activists in US history. This study serves as a bridge to identify human rights activists and issues in their own community.

Time:	Variable
Materials:	• Copies of Universal Declaration of Human Rights (UDHR) • Biographical sources such as Jacobs, W.J. *Human Rights: Great Lives,* 1990.
Setting:	Middle school – Adult groups

PROCEDURE

PART A: Activists in American History

1. If participants are not already familiar with human rights and/or the Universal Declaration of Human Rights, begin by asking participants to offer definitions of human rights. Compare their definitions with those offered in the Human Rights Glossary, p. 99. Then briefly introduce the UDHR and distribute copies of it. (See p. 3 for a background reading which might be assigned for homework). **Alternative:** show the "Animated UDHR" video from Amnesty International. (See Resource List, p. 103.)

2. Ask participants what we mean when we call someone an "activist." Record their responses. Explain that American History is filled with activists who brought significant social change. Have them generate a list from their experience. Assign each participant an activist figure to research. **Note:** Biographies for most of those listed below can be found in Jacobs, W.J. *Human Rights: Great Lives,* New York: Charles Scribner's Sons, 1990.

Ralph Abernathy	Clara Barton
Jane Addams	Ralph Bunche
Susan B. Anthony	Stokley Carmichael/Kwame Touré
Joan Baez	Cesar Chavez

Henry Cisneros	Thurgood Marshall
Dorothy Day	Harvey Milk
David Dellinger	Ralph Nader
Dorothea Dix	Rosa Parks
Frederick Douglas	Eleanor Roosevelt
W.E.B. DuBois	Jacob Riis
Mother Jones	Bayard Rustin
Chief Joseph	Elizabeth Sanger
Martin Luther King, Jr.	Mitch Snyder
William Lloyd Garrison	Elizabeth Cady Stanton
Emma Goldman	Harriet Beecher Stowe
Samuel Gompers	Dalton Trumbo
Sarah Moore & Angelina Emily Grimke	Sojourner Truth
Dolores Huerta	Booker T. Washington
Anne Hutchinson	Roger Williams
Helen Keller	Malcolm X
Winona LaDuke	John Peter Zenger
Wilma Mankiller	

3. Have each participant conduct research on her/his historical figure, obtaining basic biographical information as well as the following:

   a. causes for which the person worked;

   b. obstacles to be overcome;

   c. her/his accomplishments and influence on others;

   d. articles in the UDHR that match his/her efforts.

4. Have each participant write a summary of this research on a 5" x 8" piece of paper or card with the person's name at the top. This should include the relevant articles from the UDHR.

5. Create a list of the 30 Articles of the UDHR with a brief description of the principle, and write these on a chart or on the board. (See p. 97 for an abbreviated list.)

6. Have each participant introduce his/her historical figure without specifically naming the relevant human rights principles. The rest of the group THEN tries to match the activist's work to particular UDHR principles. When done, affix the card to the appropriate Article on the chart. Where an activist worked for more than one right, write the name next to these other articles.

7. Engage the group in a discussion of the following questions:

   • Do these activists seem to have any similar sorts of experiences and/or personal qualities. List them on the board.

   • What are some of the ways they sought to achieve their goals? Who sought to achieve goals by nonviolent means?

   • How many of them appear in school history books or your library? If so, report what is said and what is left out. How would you explain their presence or absence?

   • Introduce the definitions of civil/political and social/economic/cultural rights. (See Glossary, p. 99.) How many activists focused on social and economic rights? How many on political and civil ones?

   • If you were a human rights activist, which rights would you focus on in the United States? What human rights still need to be achieved?

   • Which articles of the UDHR have many names on the chart? How do you explain this? Which articles of the UDHR have few or none? How do you explain this?

PART B: Activists in our Community

1. Explain to participants that there are human rights activists in their local community today who are doing important work for these human rights but probably will not make it into the history textbooks. Indicate that participants will try to uncover and report on some of these local activists.

2. Brainstorm some of the human rights issues that participants recognize in their own communities today. List these on the board. Ask participants to group these into two rights categories: CIVIL/POLITICAL and SOCIAL/ECONOMIC/CULTURAL. Define these terms if necessary.

3. Brainstorm the names of local people and organizations that are working on any issues on the SOCIAL/ECONOMIC/CULTURAL list. Encourage participants to think broadly and consider school and youth organizations and activists, adult organizations and activists, faculty and staff activists, and other community institutions (e.g., religious bodies, municipal services, local chapters of national organizations) and individuals (e.g., someone who has mobilized a community project).

4. Ask participants to match the work of these local organizations and individuals with specific articles of the UDHR. Write them next to each name.

5. Have participants choose an individual or organization to research and interview. Ask them to organize their research as they did for historical figures and summarize it on a 5" x 8" card or paper. As a class or in small groups, prepare interview questions. Review and approve the questions before the interviews.

6. Have each participant report on his/her organization or individual and affix the card next to the appropriate article of the UDHR on the chart used in Part I.

Note: See Nancy Flowers (ed.), *Human Rights: Here and Now* (Minneapolis: Amnesty International USA, 1998) pp.102-104, for an expanded description of this activity.

GOING FURTHER

1. **Guest Speakers**. You may want to invite some of these activists to visit the group and speak about their work.

2. **Directory of Community Activism**. Participants might compile their research into a directory of human rights activism in their community, including contact information.

3. **Service Learning.** Individual participants or the group as a whole may wish to volunteer with some of the organizations they have learned about.

4. **Survey of School Community.** Participants might gather data on the social activism of members of their school or work community. Their findings can be added to the charts the group has begun in Parts I and II above.

Source: Written by David Shiman.

> *The new century is not going to be new at all if we offer only charity, that palliative to satisfy the conscience and keep the same old system of haves and have-nots quietly contained.*
>
> Nadine Gordimer
> 1991 Nobel Prize

Appendices

PART III CONTENTS:

Human Rights Documents

> *Where wealth is centralized, the people are dispersed.*
> *Where wealth is distributed, the people are*
> *brought together.*
>
> Confucius

UNIVERSAL DECLARATION OF HUMAN RIGHTS (UDHR)

Preamble

Whereas recognition of the inherent dignity and of the equal and inalienable rights of all members of the human family is the foundation of freedom, justice and peace in the world,

Whereas disregard and contempt for human rights have resulted in barbarous acts which have outraged the conscience of mankind, and the advent of a world in which human beings shall enjoy freedom of speech and belief and freedom from fear and want has been proclaimed as the highest aspiration of the common people,

Whereas it is essential, if man is not to be compelled to have recourse, as a last resort, to rebellion against tyranny and oppression, that human rights should be protected by the rule of law,

Whereas the peoples of the United Nations have in the Charter reaffirmed their faith in fundamental human rights in the dignity and worth of the human person and in the equal rights of men and women and have determined to promote social progress and better standards of life in larger freedom,

Whereas Member States pledged themselves to achieve, in cooperation with the United Nations, the promotion of universal respect for and observance of human rights and fundamental freedoms,

Whereas a common understanding of these rights and freedoms is of the greatest importance for the full realization of this pledge.

Now Therefore,

The General Assembly Proclaims

This Universal Declaration of Human Rights as a common standard of achievement for all peoples and all nations, to the end that every individual and every organ of society, keeping this Declaration constantly in mind, shall strive by teaching and education to promote respect for these rights and freedoms and by progressive measure, national and international, to secure their universal and effective recognition and observance, both among the peoples of Member States themselves and among the peoples of territories under their jurisdiction.

Article 1

All human beings are born free and equal in dignity and rights. They are endowed with reason and conscience and should act towards one another in a spirit of brotherhood.

Article 2

Everyone is entitled to all the rights and freedoms set forth in this Declaration without distinction of any kind, such as race, color, sex, language, religion, political or other opinion, national or social origin, property, birth or other status.

Furthermore, no distinction shall be made on the basis of the political, jurisdictional or international status of the country or territory to which a person belongs, whether it be independent, trust, non-self-governing or under any other limitation of sovereignty.

Article 3

Everyone has the right to life, liberty and security of person.

Article 4

No one shall be held in slavery or servitude; slavery and the slave trade shall be prohibited in all their forms.

Article 5

No one shall be subjected to torture or to cruel, inhuman or degrading treatment or punishment.

Article 6

Everyone has the right to recognition everywhere as a person before the law.

Article 7

All are equal before the law and are entitled without any discrimination to equal protection of the law. All are entitled to equal protection against any discrimination in violation of the Declaration and against any incitement to such discrimination.

Article 8

Everyone has the right to an effective remedy by the competent national tribunals for acts violating the fundamental rights granted him by the constitution or by law.

Article 9

No one shall be subjected to arbitrary arrest, detention or exile.

Article 10

Everyone is entitled in full equality to a fair and public hearing by an independent and impartial tribunal, in the determination of his rights and obligations and of any criminal charge against him.

Article 11

1) Everyone charged with a penal offense has the right to be presumed innocent until proved guilty according to law in a public trial at which he has had all the guarantees necessary for his defense.

2) No one shall be held guilty of any penal offense on account of any act or omission which did not constitute a penal offense, under national or international law, at the time when it was committed. Nor shall a heavier penalty be imposed than the one that was applicable at the time the penal offense was committed.

Article 12

No one shall be subjected to arbitrary interference with his privacy, family, home or correspondence, nor to attacks upon his honor and reputation. Everyone has the right to the protection of the law against such interference or attacks.

Article 13

1) Everyone has the right to freedom of movement and residence within the borders of each state.

2) Everyone has the right to leave any country, including his own, and to return to his country.

Article 14

1) Everyone has the right to seek and to enjoy in other countries asylum from persecution.

2) This right may not be invoked in the case of prosecutions genuinely arising from non-political crimes or from acts contrary to the purposes and principles of the United Nations.

Article 15

1) Everyone has the right to a nationality.

2) No one shall be arbitrarily deprived of his nationality nor denied the right to change his nationality.

Article 16

1) Men and women of full age, without any limitation due to race, nationality or religion, have the right to marry and to found a family. They are entitled to equal rights as to marriage, during marriage and at its dissolution.

2) Marriage shall be entered into only with the free and full consent of the intending spouses.

3) The family is the natural and fundamental group unit of society and is entitled to protection by society and the State.

Article 17

1) Everyone has the right to own property alone as well as in association with others.

2) No one shall be arbitrarily deprived of his property.

Article 18

Everyone has the right to freedom of thought, conscience and religion; this right includes freedom to change his religion or belief, and freedom, either alone or in community with others and in public or private, to manifest his religion or belief in teaching practice, worship and observance.

Article 19

Everyone has the right to freedom of opinion and expression; this right includes freedom to hold opinions without interference and to seek, receive and impart information and ideas through any media and regardless of frontiers.

Article 20

1) Everyone has the right to freedom of peaceful assembly and association.

2) No one may be compelled to belong to an association.

Article 21

1) Everyone has the right to take part in the government of his country, directly or through freely chosen representatives.

2) Everyone has the right of equal access to public service in his country.

3) The will of the people shall be the basis of the authority of government; this will shall be expressed in periodic and genuine elections which shall be by universal and equal suffrage and shall be held by secret vote or by equivalent free voting procedures.

Article 22

Everyone, as a member of society, has the right to social security and is entitled to realization, through national effort and international cooperation and in accordance with the organization and resources of each State, of the economic, social and cultural rights indispensable for his dignity and the free development of his personality.

Article 23

1) Everyone has the right to work, to free choice of employment, to just and favorable conditions of work and to protection against unemployment.

2) Everyone, without any discrimination, has the right to equal pay for equal work.

3) Everyone who works has the right to just and favorable remuneration ensuring for himself and his family an existence worthy of human dignity, and supplemented, if necessary, by other means of social protection.

4) Everyone has the right to form and to join trade unions for the protection of his interests.

Article 24

Everyone has the right to rest and leisure, including reasonable limitation of working hours and periodic holidays with pay.

Article 25

1) Everyone has the right to a standard of living adequate for the health and well-being of himself and of his family, including food, clothing, housing and medical care and necessary social services, and the right to security in the event of unemployment, sickness, disability, widow-hood, old age or other lack of livelihood in circumstances beyond his control.

2) Motherhood and childhood are entitled to special care and assistance. All children, whether born in or out of wedlock, shall enjoy the same social protection.

Article 26

1) Everyone has the right to education. Education shall be free, at least in the elementary and fundamental stages. Elementary education shall be compulsory. Technical and professional education shall be made generally available and higher education shall be equally accessible to all on the basis of merit.

2) Education shall be directed to the full development of the human personality and to the strengthening of respect for human rights and fundamental freedoms. It shall promote understanding, tolerance and friendship among all Nations, racial or religious groups, and shall further the activities of the United Nations for the maintenance of peace.

3) Parents have a prior right to choose the kind of education that shall be given to their children.

Article 27

1) Everyone has the right freely to participate in the cultural life of the community, to enjoy the arts and to share in scientific advancement and its benefits.

2) Everyone has the right to the protection of the moral and material interests resulting from any scientific, literary or artistic production of which he is the author.

Article 28

Everyone is entitled to a social and international order in which the rights and freedoms set forth in this Declaration can be fully realized.

Article 29

1) Everyone has duties to the community in which alone the free and full development of his personality is possible.

2) In the exercise of his rights and freedoms, everyone shall be subject only to such limitations as are determined by law solely for the purpose of securing due recognition and respect for the rights and freedoms of others and of meeting the just requirements of morality, public order and the general welfare in a democratic society.

3) These rights and freedoms may in no case be exercised contrary to the purposes and principles of the United Nations.

Article 30

Nothing in the Declaration may be interpreted as implying for any State, group or person any right to engage in any activity or to perform any act aimed at the destruction of any of the rights and freedoms set forth herein.

Adopted December 10, 1948, United Nations General Assembly

UNIVERSAL DECLARATION OF HUMAN RIGHTS
'Regular English' Version

Article 1

All human beings are born free and equal. You are worth the same, and have the same rights as anyone else. You are born with the ability to think and to know right from wrong, and should act toward others in a spirit of friendliness.

Article 2

Everyone should have all of the rights and freedoms in this statement, no matter what race, sex, or color he or she may be. It shouldn't matter where you were born, what language you speak, what religion you are, what political opinions you have, or whether you're rich or poor. Everyone should have all of the rights in this statement.

Article 3

Everyone has the right to live, to be free, and to feel safe.

Article 4

No one should be held in slavery for any reason. The buying and selling of human beings should be prevented at all times.

Article 5

No one shall be put through torture, or any other treatment or punishment that is cruel or makes him or her feel less than human.

Article 6

Everyone has the right to be accepted everywhere as a person, according to law.

Article 7

You have the right to be treated equally by the law, and to have the same protection under the law as anyone else. Everyone should have protection from being treated in ways that go against this document, and from having anyone cause others to go against the rights in this document.

Article 8

If your rights under the law are violated, you should have the right to fair and skillful judges who will see that justice is done.

Article 9

No one shall be arrested, held in jail, or thrown and kept out of her or his own country for no good reason.

Article 10

You have the same rights as anyone else to a fair and public hearing by courts that will be open-minded and free to make their own decisions if you are ever accused of breaking the law, or if you have to go to court for some other reason.

Article 11

1) If you are blamed for a crime, you have the right to be thought of as innocent until you are proven guilty, according to the law, in a fair and public trial where you have the basic things you need to defend yourself.

2) No one shall be punished for anything that was not illegal when it happened. Nor can anyone be given a greater punishment than the one that applied when the crime was committed.

Article 12

No one has the right to butt-in to your privacy, home, or mail, or attack your honesty and self-respect for no good reason. Everyone has the right to have the law protect him or her against all such meddling or attacks.

Article 13

1) Within any country you have the right to go and live where you want.

2) You have the right to leave any country, including your own, and return to it when you want.

Article 14

1) Everyone has the right to seek shelter from harassment in another country.

2) This right does not apply in cases where the person has done something against the law that has nothing to do with politics, or when she or he has done something that is against what the United Nations is all about.

Article 15

1) You have a right to a country where you're from.

2) No one should be able to take you away from, or stop you from changing your country for no good reason.

Article 16

1) Grown men and women have the right to marry and start a family, without anyone trying to stop them or make it hard because of their race, country, or religion. Both partners have equal rights in getting married, during the marriage, and if and when they decide to end it.

2) A marriage shall take place only with the agreement of the couple.

3) The family is the basic part of society, and should be protected by it.

Article 17

1) Everyone has the right to have belongings that they can keep alone, or share with other people.

2) No one has the right to take your things away from you for no good reason.

Article 18

You have the right to believe the things you want to believe, to have ideas about right and wrong, and to believe in any religion you want. This includes the right to change your religion if you want, and to practice it without anybody interfering.

Article 19

You have the right to tell people how you feel about things without being told that you have to keep quiet. You have the right to read the newspaper or listen to the radio without someone trying to stop you, no matter where you live. Finally, you have the right to print your opinions in a newspaper or magazine, and send them anywhere without having someone try to stop you.

Article 20

1) You have the right to gather peacefully with people, and to be with anyone you want.

2) No one can force you to join or belong to any group.

Article 21

1) You have the right to be part of your government by being in it, or choosing the people who are in fair elections.

2) Everyone has the right to serve her or his country in some way.

3) The first job of any government is to do what its people want it to do. This means you have the right to have elections every so often, where each person's vote counts the same, and where everyone's vote is his or her own business.

Article 22

Everyone, as a person on this planet, has the right to have her or his basic needs met, and should have whatever it takes to live with pride, and become the person he or she wants to be. Every country or group of countries should do everything they possible can to make this happen.

Article 23

1) You have the right to work and to choose your job, to have fair and safe working conditions, and to be protected against not having work.

2) You have the right to the same pay as anyone else who does the same work, without anyone playing favorites.

3) You have the right to decent pay so that you and your family can get by with pride. That means that if you don't get paid enough to do that, you should get other kinds of help.

4) You have the right to form or be part of a union that will serve and protect your interests.

Article 24

Everyone has the right to rest and relaxation, which includes limiting the number of hours he or she has to work, and allowing for holidays with pay once in a while.

Article 25

1) You have the right to have what you need to live a decent life, including food, clothes, a home, and medical care for you and your family. You have the right to get help from society if you're sick or unable to work, if you're older or a widow, or you're in any other kind of situation that keeps you from working through no fault of your own.

2) Everyone has the right to an education. It should be free of charge, and should be required for all, at least in the early years. Later education for jobs and college has to be there for anyone who wants it and is able to do it.

Article 26

1) Everyone has the right to an education. It should be free of charge, and should be required for all, at least in early years. Later education for jobs and college has to be there for anyone who wants it and is able to do it.

2) The idea of education is to help people become the best they can be. It should teach them to respect and understand each other, and to be kind to everyone, no matter who they are or where they are from. Education should help to promote the activities of the United Nations in an effort to create a peaceful world.

Article 27

1) You have the right to join in and be part of the world of art, music, and books. You have the right to enjoy the arts, and to share in the advantages that come from new discoveries in the sciences.

2) You have the right to get the credit and any profit that comes from something that you have written, made, or discovered.

Article 28

Everyone has the right to the kind of world where their rights and freedoms, such as the ones in this statement, are respected and made to happen.

Article 29

1) You have a responsibility to the place you live and the people around you-we all do. Only by watching out for each other can we each become our individual best.

2) In order to be free, there have to be laws and limits that respect everyone's rights, meet our sense of right and wrong, and keep the peace in a world where we all play an active part.

3) Nobody should use her or his freedom to go against what the United Nations is all about.

Article 30

There is nothing in this statement that says that anybody has the right to do anything that would weaken or take away these rights.

By Little House Alternative School, Dorchester, Massachusetts

UNIVERSAL DECLARATION OF HUMAN RIGHTS
(Abbreviated)

Article 1
Right to Equality

Article 2
Freedom from Discrimination

Article 3
Right to Life, Liberty, Personal Security

Article 4
Freedom from Slavery

Article 5
Freedom from Torture and Degrading Treatment

Article 6
Right to Recognition as a Person before the Law

Article 7
Right to Equality before the Law

Article 8
Right to Remedy by Competent Tribunal

Article 9
Freedom from Arbitrary Arrest and Exile

Article 10
Right to Fair Public Hearing

Article 11
Right to be Considered Innocent until Proven Guilty

Article 12
Freedom from Interference with Privacy, Family, Home and Correspondence

Article 13
Right to Free Movement in and out of the Country

Article 14
Right to Asylum in other Countries from Persecution

Article 15
Right to a Nationality and the Freedom to Change It

Article 16
Right to Marriage and Family

Article 17
Right to Own Property

Article 18
Freedom of Belief and Religion

Article 19
Freedom of Opinion and Information

Article 20
Right of Peaceful Assembly and Association

Article 21
Right to Participate in Government and in Free Elections

Article 22
Right to Social Security

Article 23
Right to Desirable Work and to Join Trade Unions

Article 24
Right to Rest and Leisure

Article 25
Right to Adequate Living Standard

Article 26
Right to Education

Article 27
Right to Participate in the Cultural Life of Community

Article 28
Right to a Social Order that Articulates this Document

Article 29
Community Duties Essential to Free and Full Development

Article 30
Freedom from State or Personal Interference in the above Rights

INTERNATIONAL COVENANT ON ECONOMIC, SOCIAL AND CULTURAL RIGHTS (ICESCR)
(Unofficial Summary)

The International Covenant on Economic, Social and Cultural Rights (1966), together with the Universal Declaration of Human Rights (1948) and the International Covenant on Civil and Political Rights (1966), make up the International Bill of Human Rights. In accordance with the Universal Declaration, the Covenants "recognize that ... the ideal of free human beings enjoying civil and political freedom and freedom from fear and want can be achieved only if conditions are created whereby everyone may enjoy his civil and political rights, as well as his economic, social and cultural rights."

Article 1

All peoples have the right of self-determination, including the right to determine their political status and freely pursue their economic, social and cultural development.

Article 2

Each State Party undertakes to take steps to the maximum of its available resources to achieve progressively the full realization of the rights in this treaty. Everyone is entitled to the same rights without discrimination of any kind.

Article 3

The States undertake to ensure the equal right of men and women to the enjoyment of all rights in this treaty.

Article 4

Limitations may be placed on these rights only if compatible with the nature of these rights and solely for the purpose of promoting the general welfare in a democratic society.

Article 5

No person, group or government has the right to destroy any of these rights.

Article 6

Everyone has the right to work, including the right to gain one's living at work that is freely chosen and accepted.

Article 7

Everyone has the right to just conditions of work; fair wages ensuring a decent living for himself and his family; equal pay for equal work; safe and healthy working conditions; equal opportunity for everyone to be promoted; rest and leisure.

Article 8

Everyone has the right to form and join trade unions, the right to strike.

Article 9

Everyone has the right to social security, including social insurance.

Article 10

Protection and assistance should be accorded to the family. Marriage must be entered into with the free consent of both spouses. Special protection should be provided to mothers. Special measures should be taken on behalf of children, without discrimination. Children and youth should be protected from economic exploitation. Their employment in dangerous or harmful work should be prohibited. There should be age limits below which child labor should be prohibited.

Article 11

Everyone has the right to an adequate standard of living for himself and his family, including adequate food, clothing and housing. Everyone has the right to be free from hunger.

Article 12

Everyone has the right to the enjoyment of the highest attainable standard of physical and mental health.

Article 13

Everyone has the right to education. Primary education should be compulsory and free to all.

Article 14

Those States where compulsory, free primary education is not available to all should work out a plan to provide such education.

Article 15

Everyone has the right to take part in cultural life; enjoy the benefits of scientific progress.

Source: Based on UN Centre on Human Rights, The International Bill of Rights, Fact Sheet #2.

A HUMAN RIGHTS GLOSSARY

CHILD LABOR: Work performed by children, often under hazardous or exploitative conditions. This does not include all work done by kids: children everywhere, for example, do chores to help their families. The 1989 UN Convention on the Rights of the Child calls for protection "against economic exploitation and against carrying out any job that might endanger well-being or educational opportunities, or that might be harmful to health or physical, mental, spiritual, moral, or social development" (Article 32).

CIVIL RIGHTS: The rights of citizens to liberty and equality (for example, freedom to access information or to vote).

CIVIL AND POLITICAL RIGHTS: The rights of citizens to liberty and equality; sometimes referred to as first generation rights. Civil rights include freedom to worship, to think and express oneself, to vote, to take part in political life, and to have access to information.

CODIFICATION, CODIFY: Process of reducing customary international law to written form.

COMMISSION ON HUMAN RIGHTS: Body formed by the ECONOMIC and SOCIAL COUNCIL (ECOSOC) of the UN to deal with human rights; one of the first and most important international human rights bodies.

CONVENTION: Binding agreement between states; used synonymously with TREATY and COVENANT. Conventions are stronger than DECLARATIONS because they are legally binding for governments that have signed them. When the UN GENERAL ASSEMBLY adopts a convention, it creates international norms and standards. Once a convention is adopted by the UN General Assembly, MEMBER STATES can then RATIFY the convention, promising to uphold it. Governments that violate the standards set forth in a convention can then be censured by the UN.

CONVENTION ON THE ELIMINATION OF ALL FORMS OF DISCRIMINATION AGAINST WOMEN (adopted 1979; entered into force 1981): The first legally binding international document prohibiting discrimination against women and obligating governments to take affirmative steps to advance the equality of women. Abbreviated CEDAW.

CONVENTION ON THE RIGHTS OF THE CHILD (adopted 1989; entered into force 1990): Convention setting forth a full spectrum of civil, cultural, economic, social, and political rights for children. Abbreviated CRC.

COVENANT: Binding agreement between states; used synonymously with CONVENTION and TREATY. The major international human rights covenants, both passed in 1966, are the INTERNATIONAL COVENANT ON CIVIL AND POLITICAL RIGHTS (ICCPR) and the INTERNATIONAL COVENANT ON ECONOMIC, SOCIAL AND CULTURAL RIGHTS (ICESCR).

CULTURAL RIGHTS: The right to preserve and enjoy one's cultural identity and development.

CUSTOMARY INTERNATIONAL LAW: Law that becomes binding on states although it is not written, but rather adhered to out of custom; when enough states have begun to behave as though something is law, it becomes law "by use"; this is one of the main source of international law.

DECLARATION: Document stating agreed upon standards but which is not legally binding. UN conferences, like the 1993 UN Conference on Human Rights in Vienna and the 1995 World Conference for Women in Beijing, usually produce two sets of declarations: one written by government representatives and one by NONGOVERNMENTAL ORGANIZATIONS (NGOs). The UN GENERAL ASSEMBLY often issues influential but legally NON-BINDING declarations.

ECONOMIC AND SOCIAL COUNCIL: A UN council of 54 members concerned principally with the fields of population, economic development, human rights, and criminal justice. This high-ranking body receives and discharges human rights reports in a variety of circumstances. Abbreviated ECOSOC.

ECONOMIC RIGHTS: Rights that concern the production, development, and management of material for the necessities of life. See SOCIAL AND ECONOMIC RIGHTS.

ENVIRONMENTAL, CULTURAL, AND DEVELOPMENTAL RIGHTS: Sometimes referred to as third generation rights, these rights recognize that people have the right to live in a safe and healthy environment and that groups of people have the right to cultural, political, and economic development.

FREE-TRADE ZONE: An industrial area in which a country allows foreign companies to import material for production and export finished goods without paying significant taxes or duties (fees to the government). A free-trade zone thus decreases a company's production costs.

HUMAN RIGHTS: The rights people are entitled to simply because they are human beings, irrespective of their citizenship, nationality, race, ethnicity, language, sex, sexuality, or abilities; human rights become enforceable when they are codified as conventions, covenants, or treaties, or as they become recognized as customary international law.

INALIENABLE: Refers to rights that belong to every person and cannot be taken from a person under any circumstances.

INDIVISIBLE: Refers to the equal importance of each human rights law. A person cannot be denied a right because someone decides it is "less important" or "non-essential."

INTERDEPENDENT: Refers to the complimentary framework of human rights law. For example, your ability to participate in your government is directly affected by your right to express yourself, to get an education, and even to obtain the necessities of life.

INTERNATIONAL BILL OF RIGHTS: The combination of these three documents: the Universal Declaration of Human Rights (UDHR), the International Covenant on Civil and Political Rights (ICCPR), and the International Covenant on Economic, Social and Cultural Rights (ICESCR).

INTERNATIONAL COVENANT ON CIVIL AND POLITICAL RIGHTS (Adopted 1966, entered into force 1976): Convention that declares that all people have a broad range of civil and political rights. One of three components of the International BILL OF RIGHTS.Abbreviated ICCPR.

INTERNATIONAL COVENANT ON ECONOMIC, SOCIAL AND CULTURAL RIGHTS (Adopted 1966, entered into force 1976): Convention that declares that all people have a broad range of economic, social, and cultural rights. One of three components of the International BILL OF RIGHTS. Abbreviated ICESCR.

INTERNATIONAL LABOR OFFICE: Established in 1919 as part of the Versailles Peace Treaty to improve working conditions and promote social justice; the ILO became a Specialized Agency of the UN in 1946. Abbreviated ILO.

MAQUILADORA: A factory, often foreign-owned, that assembles goods for export. From Spanish, the word is pronounced mah-kee-lah-DOH-rah. It is usually shortened to *maquila* (mah-KEE-lah).

MEMBER STATES: Countries that are member of the United Nations.

NON-BINDING: A document, like a DECLARATION, that carries no formal legal obligations. It may, however, carry moral obligations or attain the force of law as INTERNATIONAL CUSTOMARY LAW.

NON-GOVERNMENTAL ORGANIZATIONS: Organizations formed by people outside of government. NGO's monitor the proceedings of human rights bodies such as the COMMISSION ON HUMAN RIGHTS and are the "watchdogs" of the human rights that fall within their mandate. Some are large and international (e.g., the Red Cross, Amnesty International, the Girl Scouts); others may be small and local (e.g., an organization to advocate people with disabilities in a particular city; a coalition to promote women's rights in one refugee camp). NGO's play a major role in influencing UN policy, and many of them have official consultative status at the UN. Abbreviated NGOs.

POLITICAL RIGHTS: The right of people to participate in the political life of their communities and society such as by voting for their government.

RATIFICATION, RATIFY: Process by which the legislative body of a state confirms a government's action in signing a treaty; formal procedure by which a state becomes bound to a treaty after acceptance.

SIGN: In human rights the first step in ratification of a treaty; to sign a DECLARATION, CONVENTION, or one of the COVENANTS constitutes a promise to adhere to the principles in the document and to honor its spirit.

SOCIAL RIGHTS: Rights that give people security as they live together and learn together, as in families, schools, and other institutions.

SOCIAL AND ECONOMIC RIGHTS: Rights that give people social and economic security, sometimes referred to as security-oriented or second-generation rights. Examples are the right to food, shelter, and health care. There is disagreement whether the government is obligated to provide these benefits.

STATE: Often synonymous with "country"; a group of people permanently occupying a fixed territory having common laws and government and capable of conducting international affairs.

STATES PARTY(IES): Those countries that have RATIFIED a COVENANT or a CONVENTION and are thereby bound to conform to its provisions.

TREATY: Formal agreement between states that defines and modifies their mutual duties and obligations; used synonymously with CONVENTION. When CONVENTIONS are adopted by the UN GENERAL ASSEMBLY, they create legally binding international obligations for the member states who have signed the treaty. When a national government RATIFIES a treaty, the articles of that treaty become part of its domestic legal obligations.

UNITED NATIONS CHARTER: Initial document of the UN setting forth its goals, functions, and responsibilities; adopted in San Francisco in 1945.

UNITED NATIONS GENERAL ASSEMBLY: One of the principal organs of the UN, consisting of all member states. The General Assembly issues DECLARATIONS and adopts CONVENTIONS on human rights issues. The actions of the General Assembly are governed by the CHARTER OF THE UNITED NATIONS.

UNIVERSAL: Refers to the application of human rights to all people everywhere regardless of any distinction.

UNIVERSAL DECLARATION OF HUMAN RIGHTS (1948): Primary UN document establishing human rights standards and norms. Although the declaration was intended to be NON-BINDING, through time its various provisions have become so respected by STATES that it can now be said to be CUSTOMARY INTERNATIONAL LAW. Abbreviated UDHR.

Source: Adapted from Julie Mertus et. al., *Local Action/Global Change* and the Minnesota Partners in Human Rights *Resource Notebook*.

> *We know that a peaceful world can't long exist*
> *one-third rich and two-thirds hungry.*
>
> Jimmy Carter

RESOURCE LIST FOR
ECONOMIC, SOCIAL, AND CULTURAL RIGHTS

Print Resources

The Activists Cook Book, by Andrew Boyd
Available from: United for a Fair Economy, 37 Temple Place, 5th Floor, Boston, MA.
Tel: (617) 423-2148   Fax: (617) 423-0191   Email: stw@stw.org   <www.stw.org>

> A manual full of good ideas for taking action and making a difference on social and
> economic issues.

Children Hungering for Justice: Curriculum on Hunger and Children's Rights
Available from: Church World Service, Office on Global Education, 2115 N. Charles Street, Baltimore,
MD 21218-5755.   Tel: (410) 727-6106.

> A curriculum with units for K-1, 5-8, and high school that includes both informative activities and
> guidelines for taking action.

Child Labor is Not Cheap, by Amy Sanders
Available from: Resource Center for the Americas, 317 Seventeenth Avenue NE,
Minneapolis, MN 55414-2077.
Tel: (612) 627-9445   Fax: (612) 627-9450   Email: retamn@tc.umn.edu

> A three-lesson unit for grades 8-12 that uses innovative activities for learning about child labor
> and taking action to end it. Cost: $14.95

Exploding the Hunger Myths, by Sonja Williams
Available from: Institute for Food and Development Policy—Food First
398 60th Street, Oakland, CA 94618
Tel: (510) 654-4400   Fax: (510) 654-4551   Email: amittal@foodfirst.org

> Source of Part B of the activity *Hunger USA,* as well as other learning materials. 1987.

Food: Where Nutrition, Politics & Culture Meet, by D. Katz et. al.
Available from: Center for Science in the Public Interest
1755 S Street NW, Washington, DC 20009
Tel: (202) 332-6000

> Source of Part A of the activity *Hunger USA,* as well as other learning materials. 1976.

Human Rights for All, by Edward OBrien et. al.
Available from: Street Law Inc., 918 16th St. NW, Washington, DC 20006-2902.
Tel: (202) 293-0088   Fax: (202) 293-0089

> This comprehensive text on human rights contains a chapter on social and economic rights,
> with innovative activities and informative text. A teacher's guide in available with the text.

Listen to Us: The World's Working Children, by Jane Springer
Available from: Publishers Group West, 4054 Emeryville, CA 94608.

> This well-illustrated book helps young people understand the world. 1997.

Local Action/Global Change: Learning about the Human Rights of Women and Girls,
by Julie Mertus, Mallika Dutt and Nancy Flowers
Available from: Women's Inc., 777 UN Plaza, New York, NY 10017.
Tel: (212) 687-8633   Fax: (212) 661-2704
Email: wink@womenink.org

> This resource book has chapters and learning activities on women in the workplace, women in the economy, and the social and cultural rights of women. 1999.

The New Global Economy: A View from the Bottom Up,
Available from: Resource Center for the Americas
317 Seventeenth Avenue NE, Minneapolis, MN 55414-2077.
Tel: (612) 627-9445   Fax: (612) 627-9450   Email: retamn@tc.umn.edu   <www.americas.org/rtca>

> A 23 minute video and workshop/game kit for high school students and adults.

Sustainable America Organizer Kit on Human Rights
Available from: Sustainable America, 350 5th Ave, Room 3112, New York, NY 10118-3199.
Tel: (212) 234-4221   Fax: (202) 239-3670   Email: sustamer@sanetworkord

> A lively handbook that puts economic development in a human rights context, providing background information and action ideas. 1998.

Teaching Global Awareness with Simulation and Games, by S. Lamy et. al.
Available from: Center for Teaching International Relations, University of Denver,
2201 S Gaylord St., Denver, CO 80208.
Tel: (800) 967-2847   Fax: (303) 871-2906

> Source for "The Scramble for Wealth," and many other creative learning strategies. 1994.

Why Is There Hunger in Our Community?, by A. Dorosin, C. Geelan, E. Gordon, and R. Moore
Available from: Alameda County Community Food Bank,
10901 Russet Street, Oakland, CA 94603
Tel: (510) 568-FOOD

> Source of Part D of the activity *Hunger USA,* with curriculum units for grades K-3, 4-6, and 7-12. 1997.

Video Resources

Children without Childhoods
Available from: American Federation of Teachers Child Labor Project, 55 New Jersey Ave.,
NA, Washington, DC 20001.
Tel: (202) 879-4400   Email: online@aft.org

> One of several publications on child labor by the American Federation of Teachers.

Hunger in America
Available from: University of Illinois, Visual Aid Service, Champaign, IL 61820. Tel: (208) 333-1360.

I am a Child
Available from: International Labour Organisation, Geneva 22, 1211 Switzerland.

> A 52-minute video that offers images and personal stories of children at work. Comes with a study guide, *Stop! Child Labor.*

Kids in the Fields

Available from: The National Labor Committee, 275 7th Ave., 15th Floor, New York, NY 10001.
Tel: (212) 242-3002   Fax: (212) 242-3821   Email: nlc@nlcnet.org

An excellent 23-minute video about child farm workers.

Zoned for Slavery: The Child Behind the Label:

Available from: The National Labor Committee, 275 7th Ave., 1st Floor, New York, NY 10001.
Tel: (212) 242-3002   Fax: (212) 242-3821

A 23-minute video, used with *Child Labor is Not Cheap,* credibly esposes the plight of young workers and inspires viewers action to reform industries that rely on maquilas. 1995.

World Wide Web Resources

Human Rights Web Sites

<http://www.hrusa.org> (for curriculum/ community action ideas)

<http://www.amnesty-usa.org> (for information about Amnesty International)

<http://www.hrea.org>

<http://www.igc.org/igc/issues/hr>

<http://www.unicef.org/voy/meeting/rig/rigpico.html>

<http://www.umn.edu/humanrts>

<http://www.un.org/rights>

"A Bullet Can't Kill A Dream"   <http://www.mirrorimage.com/igbal/index.html>

American School Food Service Association   <www.asfa.org>

Bread for the World   <www.bread.org>

Campaign for Labor Rights   <www.summersault.com/-agh/clr>

Center for Economic Conversion   <www.conversion.org>

Co-op America   <www.greenpages.org> and <www.sweatshops.org>

Do Something   <www.dosomething.org>

Fair Trade Federation   <www.fairtradefederation.com>

FOOD FIRST Institute for Food & Development Policy   <www.foodfirst.org>

Free the Children   <www.freethechildren.org>

Friends Committee for National Legislation (FCNL)   <www.fcnl.org>

The Hunger Project   <www.thp.org>

International Labor Rights Fund   <www.laborrights.org>

Kensington Welfare Rights Union   <www.libertynet.org>

International Campaign to Ban Land Mines   <www.un.org/pubs/cyberschoolbus>
<www.un.org/Pubs/CSB/index.html>

National Labor Committee   <www.nlcnet.org>

Oxfam   <www.oxfamamericaorg>

People's Decade for Human Rights Education   <www.pdhre.org>

Resource Center for the Americas   <www.Americas.org/rca>

Save the Children   <www.savethechildren.org>

Sustainable America   <www.sanetwork.org>

Take Action Database   <www.react.com/activate>

UNITE! Campaign against Sweatshops   <www.uniteunion.org/sweatshops/sweatshop.html>

United for a Fair Economy   <www.stw.org>

United Nations Children's Fund (UNICEF)   <www.unicef.org/sowc96/about.htm>

US Committee for UNICEF   <www.unicefusa.org>

World Hunger Year   <www.worldhungeryear.org>

Zero Population Growth   <www.zpg.org>

ORGANIZATIONS WORKING FOR ECONOMIC AND SOCIAL JUSTICE

The following activist organizations provide resources for learning about social and economic rights.

Bread for the World
Box W, 1100 Wayne Ave, Suite 1000, Silver Springs, MD 20910
Tel: (301) 608-2400   Fax: (301) 608-2401

Bread for the World is a Christian citizens' movement that addresses hunger issues in the USA.

Campaign for Labor Rights
1247 E Street SE, Washington, DC 20003
Tel: (541) 344-5410

Publishes newsletter with up-to-date information on all sweatshop campaigns and analysis of current labor-rights issues.

Center for Economic Conversion
222 View St., Mt. View, CA 94041
Tel: (650) 968-8798   Fax: (650) 968-1126   Email: jholzman@igc.org

Educates about the military economy and facilitates the process of converting to a civilian-based economy. Resource guides, and handbooks and reports. Teacher's kit on economic conversion for high school classrooms.

Center for Teaching International Relations (CTIR)

University of Denver, 2201 S. Gaylord St., Denver, CO 80208

Tel: (800) 967-2847   Fax: (303) 871-2906

Curriculum materials and teaching guides for all grade levels, including *Teaching Global Awareness with Simulations and Games.*

Church World Service, Office on Global Education

2115 N. Charles St., Baltimore, MD 21218-5755

Tel: (410) 727-6106

Curriculum materials and fact sheets, including a curriculum available for K-12 classrooms.

Co-Op America

1612 K St. NW, #600, Washington, DC 20006

Tel: (202) 872-5307

Conducts anti-sweatshop campaigns targeting Disnet, publishes National Green Pages, <www.greenpages.org>, and sponsors <www.sweatshops.org>

Fair Trade Federation

P.O. Box 126, Barre, MA 01005

Tel: (508) 355-0284

Promotes fair-trade products and businesses.

Food First Information and Action Network

Institute for Food & Development Policy, 398 60th St., Oakland, CA 94618

Tel: (510) 654-4400

Educational materials, teaching kits, simulations, lesson plans and student readings including *Food First Curricula* that engage children in questioning the roots of global hunger.

National Labor Committee

275 Seventh Ave., 1st Floor, New York, NY 10001

Tel: (212) 242-3002   Fax: (211) 242.3821   Email: nlc@nlcnet.org   <www.nlcnet.org>

National Labor Committee provides materials on overseas sweatshops, including video entitled *Zoned for Slavery: the Child behind the Label.*

The Resource Center of the Americas

317 Seventeenth Ave. SE, Minneapolis, MN 55414-2077

Tel: (612) 627-9445   Fax: (612) 627-9450   Email: retamn@tc.umn.edu

Educational resources on economic and cultural issues in the Americas, Including *Child Labor is NOT Cheap* and *The Cost of Your Shirt,* a simulation exercise for secondary students based on the lives of Guatemalan textile workers.

Stanford Program on International and Cross-Cultural Education (SPICE)

Institute for International Studies (IIS),
Littlefield Center, Room 14, Stanford University,
300 Lasuen Street, Stanford, CA 94305-5013

Tel: (650) 723-1114

Educational resources, including *Living in a Global Age,* a simulation of international trade between developed and developing countries.

Sustainable America

42 Broadway, #1744, New York, NY 10004

Tel: (212) 239-4221

www.sanetwork.org

Email: sustamer@SANETWORK.org

> Sustainable America publishes an *Organizer Kit on Human Rights,* an action and resource kit highlighting the connection between human rights, economic rights, workers rights, and sustainable economic development.

World Bank Publications

The World Bank, P.O. Box 960, Herndon, VA 20172-0960

Tel: (703) 661-1580   (800) 645-7247   Email: books@worldbank.org

> Educational materials, including *Toward a Better World* learning kit series, providing in-depth case studies of international development projects and problems.

Zero Population Growth

1400 Sixteenth St. N.W., Suite 320, Washington, D.C. 20036

Tel: (202) 332-2200 (800) POP-1956   Fax: (202) 332-2302   Email: info@zpg.org   <www.zpg.org>

> Curriculum materials including *People and the Planet: Lessons for a Sustainable Future,* and *Earth Matters: Studies for our Global Future,* which include excellent exercises on resource use and distribution, hunger, poverty, and environmental issues.

The following activist organizations use a human rights framework, either explicitly or implicitly, in their work promoting and protecting economic, social and cultural rights. Many of their web sites provide links to similar organizations.

Center for Human Rights Education

P.O. Box 311020, Atlanta, GA 31131

Tel: (404) 344-9629   Fax: (404) 346-7517   Email: rosschre@aol.com

> CHRE trains community leaders and student activists to promote the full realization of human rights in the USA.

Clean Clothes Campaign

Minnesota Fair Trade Coalition, 317-17th Ave SE, Minneapolis, MN 55414

Tel: (612) 627-9445   Fax: (612) 627-9450

> An international campaign coalition of consumer organizations trade union, researchers and others to inform consumers about working conditions in the clothing industry and improve conditions through education and direct advocacy.

Free the Children

1750 Steele Ave. West, Suite 218, Concord, Ontario, L4K 2L7, Canada

Tel: (905) 760-9382   Fax: (905) 760-9157   Email: freechildren@clo.com   <www.freethechildren.org>

> Founded by teenager Craig Kielburger, Free the Children mobilizes young people in the fight against child labor.

Friends Committee on National Legislation (FCNL)
245 Second St., NE, Washington, DC 20002-5795
Tel: (202) 547-6000   Fax: (202) 547-6019   Email: fcnl@fcnl.org
<www.clarknet/pub/fcnl/fedbud.htm>

> The FCNL web site contains information about The Citizens Budget Campaign (CBC), a national coalition of religious, peace, and domestic human needs organizations dedicated to public education and advocacy on budget issues. Briefing papers include: Ending Hunger, Affordable Housing, Humane Welfare Policy, Sustainable Development, Economic Conversion, and Tax Justice.

The Hunger Project
15 E 26th Street, Suite 1401, New York, NY 10010
Tel: (212) 551-9100 or (800) 228-6691   Fax: (212) 532-9785   Email: jc@thp.org
<www.thp.org>

> An international organization dedicated to ending hunger by working at the grassroots level to empower individuals and teach them skills to raise themselves out of poverty.

International Child Resource Institute
1581 Leroy Ave., Berkeley, CA 94708
Tel: (510) 644-1000   Fax: (510) 525-4106   Email: ICRIChild@aol.com

> International Child Resource Institute works to improve the lives of children throughout the world by providing technical assistance and information.

Kensington Welfare Rights Union (KWRU)
PO Box 50678, Philadelphia, PA 19132-9720
Tel: (215) 763-4584   Email: kwru@libertynet.org   www.libertynet.org

> KWRU is building a movement based on and led by the interests and organization of the poor, with the goals of ending poverty and exposing violations of the right to a living wage, housing, health care, food, clothing, and education.

OXFAM
26 West Street, Boston, MA 02111
Tel: (617) 482-1211   Fax: (617) 728-2594   Email: infoforoxfamamerica.org
<www.oxfamamerica.org>

> Creates partnerships with poor communities around the world to provide emergency and technical support and program funding to break down structural barriers to self-sufficiency.

People's Decade for Human Rights Education (PDHRE)
526 11th Street, New York, NY 10025
Tel: (212) 749-3156   Fax: (212) 666-6325   Email: peopledechre@igc.org   <www.pdhre.org>

> PHDRE is a non-profit educational organization promoting the Universal Declaration's principles world wide. Their web site includes fact sheets on the human rights connection with development, work, poverty, and other economic and social issues.

Save the Children
54 Wilton Road, Westport, CN 06880
Tel: (203) 221-4024 (800) 243-5075   <www.savethechildren.org>

> Save the Children works at the community level to promote children's well-being and development.

Sweatshop Watch
310 8th St., Ste. 309, Oakland, CA 94607
Tel: (510) 834-8990   <www.sweatshopwatch.org>

A coalition committed to eliminating sweatshops.

United for a Fair Economy (formerly Share the Wealth)
37 Temple Place, 5th Floor, Boston, MA
Tel: (617) 423-2148   Fax: (617) 423-0191   Email: stw@stw.org   <www.stw.org>

United for a Fair Economy draws public attention to the consequences of growing income and wealth inequality, through educational programs such as *The Activist Cookbook,* development of organizing tools, action campaigns, and research.

U.S. Committee for UNICEF
333 E. 38th St., New York, NY 10016
Tel: (212) 686-5522   Email: webmaster@unicefusa.org   <www.unicefusa.org>

U.S. Committee for UNICEF works in more than 160 countries and territories proving health care, clean water, improved nutrition, and education.

World Hunger Year
505 Eighth Ave, 21st floor
New York, NY 10018-6582
Tel: (212) 629-8850 or (800) 5-HUNGRY   Email:whyear@aol.com   <www.worldhungeryear.org>

World Hunger Year was created to support and promote innovative, long term solutions to hunger through self-reliance, economic justice, community building, and food security.

SUBJECT INDEX